RESUMES
THAT GET
JOBS

RESUMES
THAT GET
JOBS

Jean Reed

Prentice Hall
New York • London • Toronto • Sydney • Tokyo • Singapore

Sixth Edition

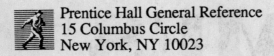 Prentice Hall General Reference
15 Columbus Circle
New York, NY 10023

Copyright © 1992 by Arco Publishing, a division
of Simon & Schuster, Inc.

An Arco Book

Arco, Prentice Hall, and colophons are
registered trademarks of Simon & Schuster, Inc.

Library of Congress Cataloging-in-Publication Data

Reed, Jean.
Resumes that get jobs / Jean Reed.—6th ed.
    p. cm.
Includes index.
ISBN 0-13-755430-3
1. Résumés (Employment) 2. Applications for positions.
I Title.
HF5383.G725   1992   92-13784
650.14—dc20   CIP

Manufactured in the United States of America

1 2 3 4 5 6 7 8 9 10

CONTENTS

PART 1
ESSENTIAL INFORMATION

PART 2
SAMPLE RESUMES

PART 3
OCCUPATIONAL OUTLOOK 2000

RESUME INDEX

Part 1

Essential Information

ABOUT RESUMES
AND THE JOB SEARCH PROCESS

What Is a Resume?

Résumé —pronounced *REZ-oo-may*—is a French word meaning "summary."
Although many dictionaries spell the word with accents, it is acceptable to drop
them, as is done in this book.

For the job applicant, a resume has become an indispensable tool. A good
resume can be the most important factor in determining whether a prospective
employer decides to call you in for an interview. In short, a well-prepared resume
may literally get you a foot in the door.

An accurate, detailed resume serves another important function. It serves as a
point of reference during the interview, as well as an advantageous focal point for
conversation between you and the prospective employer.

How to Use Your Resume for Finding Jobs

An obvious, but limited, use of your resume is to send it where you know an
opening exists. There are, however, other ways to use it. For example, you can use
your resume in any of the following situations:

Seek Out Your Own Openings. If a firm, company, or organization is
particularly appealing to you, send the firm your resume even though there is no
apparent opening. Find out all you can about the operation in order to sound
knowledgeable in your cover letter. Get an executive's name to send your resume
to (use the telephone), and go to the top if necessary. Letters that are "handed
down" get attention. Many good career opportunities are never advertised, and
you will immediately garner points for eagerness and initiative. If you are
presently employed, be cautious if the firm is in the same town as yours, and stress
confidentiality. It's usually respected, but be aware that there is no guarantee.

Employment Agencies. There is a big push to upgrade state agencies and the
quality of job orders. Tax-paying employers are beginning to realize that they are
paying for these services, and more and more are taking advantage of them. Job
seekers are the beneficiaries, so don't ignore these free services that are yours for
the asking.

Private agencies can be expensive as well as unproductive. Ask tough questions
about fees and their policy if you quit or get dismissed from any job they obtain
for you. Insist on firm, exact replies. Read what you sign, including the fine print.

Help-Wanted Advertisements. These columns are often scrutinized by employment agencies, who will call the advertiser and say, "I've got a person qualified for this job." The columns are equally available to you at no charge. At certain levels they can be productive with a good resume and cover letter. If you already have a job, be cautious of blind ads. They could have been placed by your employer.

Search Firms ("Headhunters"). The search firm's function is to match client qualifications to job openings in a wide range of fields. Search firms don't advertise as a rule, but many will review unsolicited resumes, especially if you are in, say, upwards of a $35,000 salary bracket and have a good record of achievement. Check your local library for lists of search firms and their specialties. You may find one that matches your objective.

RESUME FORMAT

While no two people agree on the exact form and content of a resume, there is a sizeable area of full agreement among employers and personnel people. This book will teach you to write the type of resume that will appeal to the people who count—those who will read the resume. The form of resume presented has been uniformly accepted by employers the nation over as concise, informative, and clear.

You will note that the first page of our resume format is a synopsis (or condensation) of the amplification that follows. This form has a distinct advantage. It enables an employer to tell at a glance whether or not he or she wants to know more about you. If the employer likes what is in the synopsis, he or she will be eager to read the amplification that follows. If the employer does not care for what is in the synopsis, you have saved everybody's time.

Following is a skeleton resume to show the basic resume form. It is practical because it is flexible. You will see that infinite variations are possible. For example, if your position is more impressive than the company name, reverse placement of "title" and "company name." However, for the sake of appearance, be consistent and follow this procedure for all employments listed. If you have an excellent education, and employment has been part-time or relatively unimportant, reverse the position of "Experience" and "Education." You will have to decide for yourself what is most important to the person who is going to read your resume.

Synopsis of Resume:

JOHN DOE
Street Address
City, State, Zip Code
(area code) phone number

JOB OBJECTIVE:

EXPERIENCE:

Dates (start–end)	Name of Company, Address of Company
Present or last company	Type of Business
	Job Title

Dates (start–end)	Name of Company, Address of Company
	Type of Business
	Job Title

**MISCELLANEOUS
EXPERIENCE:** Grouping of part-time and/or minor employments

EDUCATION:

Dates (start–end)   College—location
Degree: Major: Minor:
[Class standing—insert if superior]*
[Honors:]
[Expenses: percentage earned]
[Activities: extracurricular]

Dates (start–end)   High School—location
Note: unnecessary if college is shown

**MISCELLANEOUS
EDUCATION:** Company courses; correspondence courses;
seminars; home study

INTERESTS: What you do for recreation

AFFILIATIONS: [Optional, unless job-related]

(FOR AMPLIFICATION, SEE FOLLOWING.)

Items in brackets are optional.

Amplified Resume:

EMPLOYMENT HIGHLIGHTS

Date of starting to present
FULL NAME OF LAST OR PRESENT COMPANY

    Responsibilities:

    Results:

    Reason for leaving:

Date of starting to date of leaving
FULL NAME OF COMPANY

    Responsibilities: (less detailed)

    Results: (less detailed)

    Reason for leaving:

Date of starting to date of leaving
FULL NAME OF COMPANY

    Responsibilities: (Note: If resume is in proper sequence,
    Results: this and ensuing employments will usually
    Reason for leaving: be of less importance and correspondingly
                                   less detailed.)

MISCELLANEOUS EMPLOYMENTS
Dates can be approximate, but should indicate
frame of period involved.

    Group your minor (miscellaneous) employments, stating in general the type of
    work. If you are under 25, group your part-time employments, particularly
    during school years.

    <u>Example:</u>
    1989–90   Self-employed. Mowed lawns.
    1991–92   McDonald's Restaurant. Busperson.

References on request.

WHAT TO PUT ON YOUR RESUME

Job Objective

The job objective is the "soul" of your resume and should be given first and foremost consideration. It should say what you want to do as clearly and concisely as possible.

Decide on the type of job for which you are best equipped by reason of your temperament, personal preferences, capabilities, and experience—then state it. If it is in sales, what kind? Is management your goal? Any travel restrictions? This would then be stated,"Position in sales leading to management. Prefer limited travel." Note examples on the actual resumes in this book. Unless you have strong geographical preferences, do not state them, as this serves only to narrow the scope of your availability.

Suppose you do not have very definite or well-defined objectives; or perhaps you have several. You may consider comprehensive job counseling, or at least discuss your background with an employment counselor to determine the best statement of your objectives. In any event, we urge you to avoid the "all-purpose—will do anything" type of objective. You cannot sell a product successfully unless you are specific about its advantages to the buyer.

Employment

List employment in reverse chronological order (your present or last job *first*, etc.). Be certain you list starting and leaving dates, your position title, the exact name of the company, and its present address. If the company has changed name or address since you were there, state "Jones-Smith Co., 114 Main St., Newark, NJ (formerly known as Smith Co., 90 South Ave., Camden, NJ)." "Type of business" is for purposes of identification only and is not necessary when the company is well known nationally, or if identification is obvious from the company name, as in "Morris *Lumber* Company."

To state salary is to lose your bargaining power. At the interview, your salary will, and *must*, be discussed. However, for resume purposes, showing the percentage of increase (if noteworthy) in the amplification portion is a safe middle road to travel. At the executive level, you might say "salary in low, middle, or high five figures" to establish your level without pinpointing the exact amount. This can appear in one line of the synopsis page.

Education

The farther you are from school, the less educational detail you need to provide. Use the form shown on page 5 to set forth your education clearly and concisely—fitting it, of course, to your particular situation. Make certain that the names and locations of schools and the dates attended are correct, especially if you can list fairly recent courses to show a continued effort at self-improvement.

Recent graduates have little but education for sale. Therefore they should cover this area thoroughly, listing not only their majors and minors, but any and all subjects related to their fields of interest. They might also list semester hours and grades when better than average. Extracurricular activities are important, for they indicate a well-rounded personality and demonstrate social awareness. This importance, of course, diminishes with time—so again, the older you are, and the farther away from school, the fewer items you should list.

Work during college for the recent graduate can be shown on the synopsis page under "Experience," and/or the Amplification part of your resume (see page 6) as space permits.

Do *not* omit your education because it is limited. Expand upon it where possible by listing company courses, home-study courses, etc. This indicates a desire for self-education readily understood by the often sympathetic employer, who (like you) may not have had the opportunity for extensive formal education. The same employer will not be equally sympathetic to amateurish attempts at bluffing an education you do not have.

Interests/Affiliations

Interests flesh out your portrait, so by all means include them. A word of warning: Do not give yourself a fanciful interest in an attempt to impress. A good interviewer will nail you for it, and it's a silly way to lose a good career opportunity.

Affiliations, particularly when job-related, can serve to put the finishing touches to your word picture. Community involvement as indicated by partici-pation in Rotary, United Way, Shriners, or other organizations is positive input.

Military Service

If service is recent and extensive, it can be on the synopsis page and amplified. Otherwise, a lone line regarding it will suffice.

The recently discharged servicemember (like the recent graduate) has little but service experience, education, and training to sell and should give these emphasis. Generally speaking, select the functions you performed most capably and relate them to a civilian occupation field.

Analysis of Amplification Preparation

Before discussing how to write the details of your history, it is necessary to review briefly just what a resume is. A resume is, in essence, a piece of direct mail advertising—*and the product is YOU*.

Effective direct mail advertising is: (1) attractive in appearance; (2) provocative in content; and (3) positive in approach. Emphasis is *always* on what the product has done and is capable of doing, *never* on what it has not done and why. Keep this foremost in your mind when preparing your own "direct mail advertising."

The sole purpose of a resume is to arouse interest and to get you an interview. Save some ammunition for that interview, but get enough into the resume to make the interviewer want to know more about you—to call you in and talk with you. Strive to sound like a good investment.

Responsibilities

State in what capacity you were employed and what you were expected to do. Also state level of responsibility. Use phrases like "completely responsible for." Many jobs involve familiarity with certain kinds of equipment or processes. For instance, in data processing, state any equipment within your experience and what you are able to do with it, such as operate or program; in purchasing, state type of materials, components, etc., that you were responsible for purchasing; in manufacturing, state the kinds of equipment involved; and so on.

If your most recent job represents your highest skills (as it probably does), give it the most space. If it has resulted from a definite progression from earlier jobs, such jobs can be covered more briefly.

Results

This is the body of your resume, for here you have set yourself apart from the herd through accomplishment. Everyone has responsibilities, but not everyone fulfills them to the same degree. Results give you stature above and beyond a formal (and sometimes meaningless) title bestowed on you by a firm. Again, remember the advertising approach. Point up what you can do by showing what you have done. You must sell your value to a company as deftly and effectively as it sells its products to the public. For example, if you are a salesperson, alert the employer to the fact that you are a good one by the simple expedient of showing increased sales volume. Perhaps you only maintained sales volume but did so under unusual difficulties. State what they were and how you overcame them.

In many fields, results cannot be measured in so simple a fashion. However, salary increases, promotions, and increased responsibilities all can be "results."

You might have received recognition in the form of an award. You might have completed a project outside the framework of your responsibilities and received no particular recognition for it; reward yourself in your resume by stating what you did. If necessary, list such extracurricular activity under the heading "Special Accomplishments."

If you have been with one firm for a long time, it is sometimes difficult to show concrete results. Employ the "progression" technique. The principle involved here is simple. To have started as a delivery boy and to have ended up as a file clerk makes you a more important file clerk.

Miscellaneous or Part-Time Work Details

State what you did in general terms (selling, construction, general office work), but where possible state the name of the company. This gives credence to your statements. Also make certain you give the approximate dates this miscellaneous work period covered. The purpose of this grouping is twofold: (1) it shortens your resume yet still accounts for all your working years, and (2) it avoids the impression of job-hopping.

Reason for Leaving

Ordinarily the reason for leaving should be given for each employment you list. Don't get involved or verbose. A simple phrase will often do.

On the other hand, at times the reason for leaving cannot be stated tersely because it came about through a complex situation involving other people, kind of work, rate of pay, and other factors. Try to tell your story clearly and concisely, avoiding phrases that reflect unfavorably upon you—such as "No chance for advancement." (Why did you take the job in the first place?) Substitute "To advance career progression" or "To work in growth environment."

If your reason for leaving was a battle with your boss, say "To seek position where professional standards mesh with corporate policy." It sounds less peevish than "Disagreement with management." If you left because your pay remained the same for too long, try "To seek position commensurate with skills and experience." It says more for you than "No salary increase."

Eventually, an employer will probably want to cover these matters thoroughly, but for resume purposes, brevity without bitterness is the rule. If all else fails, say that the reason for leaving is "to be discussed at interview."

Length of Resume

It is not advisable to make arbitrary statements on resume length. Length will vary to the same degree that individual records vary. However, the average record can be handled satisfactorily in two pages (counting the synopsis sheet as one).

Occasionally a complex or highly varied record requires a third page to tell the story properly and to avoid overcrowding. If employers like what they see at a glance, their appetite is whetted for detail; therefore, they proceed with an eye to content rather than page number. For practical purposes, a good rule of thumb is two-page minimum, three-page maximum.

References

Unless references are requested, most employers are unimpressed by such a list. There are two good reasons for this: (1) Any name you list is obviously a friend, understandably prejudiced in your favor, and (2) the word of a past employer is not necessarily significant. Prospective employers are aware that it is not an uncommon practice for a past employer to give a likeable yet unsatisfactory worker a break in the form of a good reference. These and other factors serve to render the reference list of little or no value. For resume purposes, stating "References available" is a a safe, standard, and acceptable practice.

You may disagree. If so, there is no harm in listing your references. However, this probably does little good in the resume itself.

Physical Preparation of Resume

Just as you are not inclined to buy a product in a soiled wrapper, an employer does not "buy" you on cheap paper, messy with erasures and misspelled words. There are several acceptable ways for you to physically prepare your resume. First, you may choose to have it typeset by a professional typesetting/printing business service. Resumes done this way are certainly attractive and professional-looking; however, they can be quite expensive to produce. Preparing your resume on a word processor, or having it prepared by a professional using one, is generally less expensive than having it typeset—and word processors can create resumes that are as attractive as typeset ones. Finally, it is always acceptable to type your resume on a traditional typewriter—just be neat. Whichever method you choose for preparing your resume, use our basic format. Then make photocopies of your original resume on good bond paper. The cost per page for copying a two- to three-page resume 50 to 100 times is relatively inexpensive—and since your position may hinge upon it, it is money well spent.

Resist all suggestions or advice to use a marker pen on your resume for emphasis. Proper emphasis is achieved in a resume by clear format and concise, meaty content. Colored underscoring and marginal notes are childish.

Do not use a resume cover. A few die-hards still persist in encasing their typed resumes in expensive cardboard or vinyl covers. Don't be one of them. It's the mark of an amateur, a showoff, or both. More importantly, prospective employers are irritated by covers; they don't fit in a resume file. They do fit in "the circular file."

ANSWERING CLASSIFIED ADS

"Wanted: mature, responsible, full-time salesperson. Respond to P.O. Box 123, Milltown, NY 12345."

It is assumed that you have armed yourself with a good resume before answering a classified advertisement. The next step is writing a specific cover letter. Specific ad-answering technique does not vary appreciably from the technique of writing any good covering letter of application, except for one point: follow the advertisement line so that you will sound tailor-made for the job. See the first sample cover letter, on page 13, which is slanted to the above advertisement.

GENERAL COVER LETTERS

Always enclose a cover letter when you mail out a resume.

Cover letters should be individually typed and signed. Anything else indicates a serious lack of interest, and a lack of elementary business courtesy as well.

Your cover letter should be brief and follow these general guidelines. See the second sample letter, on page 14.

1. Address your letter to a specific person. Employers are people, and people tend to be complimented when you know their names and titles. It's worthwhile to make an effort to find this information out.

If the company you are applying to is located nearby, phone the main switchboard and ask for the name of the sales manager, director of human resources, or other appropriate person. It's not necessary to identify yourself or your reason for calling. If you should be pressed, a disarming "I want to write him (her) a letter" will usually do the trick.

Sample Cover Letter #1

Ms. Elinor Adison
123 Cherry Lane
Milltown, NY 12345

August 10, 1992

P.O. Box 123
Milltown, NY 12345

Dear Sir or Madam:

Your advertisement in the August 9th issue of the *Daily News* emphasized your need for a mature, responsible salesperson. I offer department store sales experience and consider my professionalism to be one of my greatest strengths. I am free to accept a full-time position and have no objection to overtime or weekend work if required.

My track record in sales is described on the attached resume. Thank you for your consideration.

Sincerely,

(handwritten signature)

Eleanor Adison

Sample Cover Letter #2

Ms. Lois Gunther
1877 Orange Avenue
Sarasota, FL 33579

October 11, 1992

Mr. George Howe
Manager, Howe Realtors
29 Prospect Street
Sarasota, FL 33581

Dear Mr. Howe:

Having recently acquired my Florida real estate license, I know that working for your highly respected company would be the ideal means of learning the practical sales skills needed to supplement enthusiasm and education.

I offer extensive neighborhood contacts, which I established during my previous employment in the Lee County school system. My ability to network in the local community is certain to generate sales for your realty firm. In addition, my familiarity with mortgage brokering will help you close sales quickly and efficiently.

I enclose my resume and will call your office next week to request an interview. Thank you for your consideration.

Sincerely,

(handwritten signature)

Lois Gunther

(A generally good approach when sending out a resume "cold," i.e., without any knowledge that an opening may exist. Requires a bit more "self-sell" to generate interest in reading the resume.)

Synopsis of Resume:

LOIS GUNTHER
1877 Orange Avenue
Sarasota, FL 33579
(803) 922-0778

JOB OBJECTIVE:	Real Estate Salesperson

EDUCATION:

1991   **Principles and Practices of Real Estate**
St. Lawrence College (extension)

Other: **Real Estate License Law Course**
Reagon Specialized School of Instruction

License: **Florida Real Estate Salesperson's License**
Received November 1983
Notary-Public-at-Large, State of Florida
Commission valid through 1987

College: **University of Florida**
B.A. in History

EXPERIENCE:

10/90–Present   **Boomhower Real Estate Company**
Arcadia, Florida

10/89–10/90   **Lindsey Title and Mortgage**
Miami, Florida

1987–89   **Lee County Schools**, Ft. Myers, Florida
History Teacher

Other: General office work, sales

INTERESTS: Sports car rallying; sewing; reading

AFFILIATIONS: Sarasota Board of Realtors
Florida Board of Realtors
National Board of Realtors

(FOR AMPLIFICATION, SEE FOLLOWING.)

*(Note: Ms. Gunther is changing fields; consequently she deemphasizes her former profession
in favor of her newly acquired education in her present field, and she focuses on
the sales aspect of her former record—a needed tool in the new field.)*

Amplified Resume:

EMPLOYMENT HIGHLIGHTS

October 1990–Present
BOOMHOWER REAL ESTATE COMPANY

Accepted position as salesperson with assurance of participation in planned sales training program under guidance of an experienced member of the sales force.

Program failed to materialize; seeking to make change to company that would provide background training in the practical aspects of selling to complement and embellish theories and principles learned in acquiring recent real estate license.

October 1989–October 1990
LINDSEY TITLE AND MORTGAGE

Accepted position as mortgage clerk to obtain practical experience in real estate field. Responsible for shipping out recorded closing instruments and typing of title insurance policies.

Given occasional opportunities to go into field for sales indoctrination and found this to be best area and ultimate goal.

Reason for leaving: To accept sales training leading to full-time sales position with major firm above.

1987–89
LEE COUNTY SCHOOLS

Taught History at junior high level; also responsible for school library.

During the summer of 1988, accepted position as manager of the Taylor Galleries in Ft. Myers. Among other responsibilities, managed sales promotion of rare paintings, sculpture, and sundry objets d'art. Customers ranged from general tourists to visiting dignitaries.

Handled all books and relevant correspondence; closed sales. Offered year-round position following; unable to accept.

References on request.

If the job is important enough, this call should be made wherever the company is located. Don't rely on some friend's recollection of a name or on personnel records. These records get out of date rapidly, and a letter addressed to a predecessor immediately labels you as a person with a certain carelessness for meaningful detail.

2. Your letter need not cover the same ground as your resume. It should merely sum up what you have to offer and act as an introduction for your resume.

3. Let your letter reflect your individuality, but avoid appearing familiar, overbearing, humorous, or cute.

4. With local firms, take the initiative in suggesting that you telephone for an interview.

5. With out-of-town or out-of-state firms, it is imperative that you indicate willingness to travel for a personal interview. Better yet, give dates when you could be in the area for one.

HOW EMPLOYERS READ RESUMES

Thomas McElheny, Ph.D., the author of this article, is the founder of the American Center for Management and Professional Development, which develops management seminars for the major Fortune 500 companies. He is currently Chairman and CEO of the Christian Purchasing Network, Inc., which has a $30 million volume.

The first thing I look for in a resume is problem-solving ability—the ability to create solutions as opposed to creating problems. I am not so concerned that someone has worked at a place for seven or eight years. At the same time, I don't want to see a pattern of change every six months. There has to be a reasonable in-between.

I look at the positions held. For example, "shipping clerk." That title is not descriptive in and of itself. Our shipping clerk is a person who has to think on his feet, solve problems, and make decisions. Another shipping clerk may be someone who carries boxes from point A to point B. Consequently, I don't accept just the job title. I want to see the work detailed in the resume.

I look for character. Integrity and commitment are important to me. A tip-off of lack of commitment would be excessive changing of jobs. If the change is obviously to improve status, yes. But if a person has been trained by a company and quits on a whim, that's cheating.

I am turned off by incomplete information. When I read "B.S." or "college degree," I want to know what school, what year, what was your major. At the same time, don't kill me with details such as "President of Drama Club."

I like enough personal information to get an accurate visual picture. For example, a former officer in the armed services would mean to me presence, assertiveness, and leadership qualities. I highly endorse listing interests on a resume and I ask about them to make sure they are not there just to impress me.

I am offended when I feel the resume is written in an attempt to manipulate me. Don't try to hide your age from me. If you've had twenty-five years of hands-on experience, it tells me you're no kid, but in a positive way.

On the other hand, if an applicant takes the time to find out about my organization, our needs and requirements, and sends me a resume slanted to that extent, I am not offended. I am flattered.

We hire speakers, and I receive perhaps twenty-five resumes a week [for these jobs]. The first thing I do is turn everybody down four times. If they don't have the innate persistence to do whatever it takes to get to me, I'm not interested.

Secondly, I look at the personality of the applicant to see if it matches my needs. To be a speaker you have to have academic credentials, but there is a way to say you're an expert without being an ass.

The key characteristic for a platform speaker is to be able to keep an adult audience interested in your topic for eight hours a day, three days on end. It requires high levels of energy, interest, and knowledge. I look for that.

When I get a package of eighty-two pages of articles an applicant wrote, it tells me that he or she doesn't know very much about this business.

The distinctive resume that jumps out at me is the resume that pinpoints a candidate's ability to give a good presentation. I don't care if applicants are 110 pounds or 200 pounds if they can utilize their image to give a good presentation. One of my best speakers is not very attractive physically, but he's a huggy teddy bear. He's taken his physical attributes and maximized the impact.

His resume was to the point and the references he listed were well-known, good people in the field. Normally, references do not impress me at all, especially on the standard job resume. The only form I find acceptable is "On Request."

Prior salary levels do not turn me off at all. If someone is honest enough to tell me what he or she made, there are trade-offs. I may be paying less with more opportunity. Nevertheless, I think I'd leave salary off a job resume. A resume is a selling tool, and in selling, the idea is to create interest but not to give so much information you kill the sale.

I like affiliations too. I like the fact that an applicant is involved with the United Way and various community organizations. The evidence is that there is something in life more important than his or her own concerns. People whose focus is entirely on themselves eventually are going to crash.

INTERVIEW STRATEGY

Questions You Can Be Asked During the Interview

Name and Address. You must give your name and address, and can be asked how long you've resided at that address or in your employer's city and state. You can be asked whether you have worked for that company under a different name, changed your name, or ever used an assumed name, so that the employer can check your previous work record.

Work Experience. You can be asked for names and addresses of previous employers, previous job duties, the length of time you held the job, your promotions, and your reasons for leaving.

Education. You can be asked about your educational background in detail.

Convictions for Crime. You can be asked whether you have ever been convicted of a crime and for the details. You cannot be asked about arrests—only convictions.

Questions You Should Not Be Asked During an Interview

The law says when you apply for a job you cannot be discriminated against because of your race, color, national origin, religion, gender, age, and in some cases, physical or mental handicaps.

This sounds straightforward, but unfortunately, it isn't always so clear. However, employers and applicants must carry on, trying to live within both the federal laws and the state antibias laws, and the following guidelines have been developed as to how sensitive topics should be handled to avoid conflict with federal and state laws.

Race or Color. Neither should be the subject of any comment in an interview, and you should not be asked for a picture of yourself when you apply for a job.

National Origin. You should not be asked about your national origin, lineage, ancestry, or descent, or that of your spouse, unless the employer is an organization promoting a particular national heritage.

Religion. You should not be asked about your religious background or beliefs. Your religious convictions could be relevant to a job (a workweek that might violate your religious ethic, for example). But the employer cannot raise the issue by asking about your religion or by suggesting that you might object to the job for that reason.

Gender and Marital Status. Beyond a clear-cut example such as a commercial actor, gender should not enter into the hiring process. You should not be asked about your marital status, whether your spouse works, or even whom you would like notified in case of an emergency. Questions about children, child-care arrangements, likelihood of pregnancy, and your views on birth control are similarly off limits.

Age. As long as you are an adult under seventy years of age, your age should be irrelevant, unless age enters into the specific function of the job. For example, let's say the job is that of a smoke jumper who jumps out of airplanes to fight forest fires. There has been reasonable medical evidence that anyone over forty cannot do this without an extraordinary increase in risk. In this case the employer can discriminate against anyone over forty, not just you. Airlines were not successful in establishing that persons over a certain age were not able to fulfill flight attendant functions; consequently, their hard-and-fast age rule went by the board.

Handicaps. Federal laws prohibit employers from discrimination in hiring on the basis of physical or mental handicaps. Once an employer has detailed the requirements of a job, he or she can ask you whether you have any physical or mental problems that would preclude your satisfactorily performing the job.

Commonly Asked Interview Questions and How to Answer Them

1. *Tell me something about yourself.*

Know your resume details and state them concisely.

2. *Why do you want to work for us?*

Do any research possible ahead of time to be ready for this question. Explain that you are impressed with the company's policies, reputation, working conditions, physical plant—whatever seems germane.

3. *Why should I hire you?*

Because you are uniquely qualified and your personal goals coincide with the employer's. Explain what you can bring to the job.

4. *Why did you leave your last job?*

Your answer should reflect what is said on your resume.

5. *Why are you thinking of leaving your present job?*

Be honest, be brief, but be diplomatic. Do not baldly cite reasons such as "I want more money," "I'm sick of office politics," or "I can't stand the pressure." Try "To broaden my experience," "To advance into management," or "To obtain a position equal to my experience and skill."

6. *What are your strengths?*

Careful study of your resume in advance will prepare you for this question, plus help you document your reply. Does it reveal leadership? Ambition? Loyalty? Determination? Ability to work under pressure? To cope? To get along with people? Steady work record? Extraordinary abilities (sales, administrative, etc.)?

7. *What are your weaknesses?*

You can turn this question to your advantage by thinking it through ahead of time. For example, "I expect my co-workers to have the same strong work ethic I do," "I'm impatient to get things done," or "I'm intolerant of poor-quality work."

8. *Where do you expect to be ten or twenty years from now?*

This is a favorite. Think it through carefully and resist all temptations to make a flip response. "In your job" can be a dangerous reply to an insecure man or woman. It's safe to say that you expect promotions and salary increases in line with your productivity.

9. *What is the minimum salary you would find acceptable?*

Know the salary range of the job and inquire whether this is in line with the company's scale. Stress job satisfaction and willingness to accept a starting figure you can genuinely live with. Negotiate if necessary.

10. *When could you start work here?*

If not working—immediately! If working, play fair with your present employer—a week to two weeks' notice if in a nonsupervisory capacity; one month minimum in a management or supervisory capacity.

Questions You Should Ask
a Prospective Employer

1. What would my duties and responsibilities be? A large firm may have a prepared job description. Ask for it.

2. If salary has not yet been discussed, broach it in the same manner discussed under interviewer questions.

3. Whom will I be working for and with? What will my hours be?

4. What are my opportunities for advancement? Raises?

5. What are my opportunities for additional training and/or education?

6. What are your employee benefits? How soon after hiring would I be eligible to use them?

7. What are your (company/firm/store) policies on: holidays, lunch, dress, smoking, coffee breaks?

8. Are employees paid every week, every two weeks, or on the 15th and 30th of the month? Does your (company/firm/store) withhold the first paycheck?

9. Can I provide you with any additional information to help you evaluate me for this position?

10. May I ask when I can expect a decision regarding this position?

COURTESY AFTER THE INTERVIEW

According to corporate personnel directors, only one percent of job applicants follow up an interview with a letter of thanks. Often they are among the chosen few who get job offers, because this simple, courteous gesture makes them stand out from the rest.

The smart job applicant will send a brief thank-you letter the same day as the interview, or at the latest, the day after the interview. See the letter on page 23 for an example.

This letter may be handwritten only if your handwriting is excellent. If you need to type it and don't own a typewriter, enlist the aid of a friend or business service. You might check whether your local public library or public school offers the use of typewriters or word processors.

THE INTERVIEW FROM THE EMPLOYER'S VIEWPOINT

This is the philosophy and strategy used in screening resumes and conducting employment interviews by Vincent M. Tarduogno, Vice President of Regional Market Planning for Merrill, Lynch, Pierce, Fenner, & Smith in Princeton, New Jersey. Mr. Tarduogno has conducted "Employee Selection and Hiring Practices" seminars at the University of South Florida and is currently a member of the Business Administration Advisory Council at Trenton State College; he holds an M.B.A. from Michigan State University.

Initial employment screening is, of course, done through resumes. I expect a resume to be clean, easy to read, and on quality paper. I like the content to flow and to give me an overview of the person, starting with his or her most recent experience and working backward.

I like some verbiage on what has been accomplished within a particular job, and I look for consistency in job change, and that there are no lapses in time. I look for stability. For example, are there a lot of restless jumps in jobs, or do the

Sample Thank-You Letter

Ms. Lois Gunther
1877 Orange Avenue
Sarasota, FL 33579

November 3, 1992

Mr. George Howe
Manager, Howe Realtors
29 Prospect Street
Sarasota, FL 33581

Dear Mr. Howe:

I want to express my thanks to you for the time and courtesy extended to me today. After learning about the exciting career opportunities in your firm I am even more enthusiastic about working for Howe Realtors.

I believe my interests and capabilities would permit me to make some valuable contributions to your sales team, to our mutual benefit.

I will telephone you in several days for your decision. Thank you for your consideration.

Sincerely,

(handwritten signature)

Lois Gunther

applicants move from job to job in a logical fashion? What kinds of choices have they made in their lives? Why have they made these choices? Is the new job significantly better?

I like enough personal information to get a verbal snapshot. In short, lay out a clear picture of yourself, but don't volunteer negative information. Education should be included, but if you have less than a 3.0 grade average in college, don't bother putting it on a resume. Most good interviewers have a sixth sense, and they'll catch you at it.

The biggest turnoff to me is not being able to follow chronologically on a resume, and using the functional approach such as "selling skills," "managerial skills," etc. This is too involved for a resume. That's for me to find out in the interview. All I'm looking for is to have my appetite whetted as to whether I have an interest in pursuing this person further.

As to the actual interview, I think the question "Tell me about yourself" is a bad interview question. It is a stress-inducing question and the job of good interviewer is to put the candidate at ease.

Nonetheless, if someone asks you that stressful question, you almost have to answer it, so be prepared. Make notes and rehearse at home so that under stress you won't blurt out some negative information in a nervous compulsion to fill the silence.

On an initial interview, I ask why applicants want to make a change and why they think they would like to work for us. This way I find out if they have a reasonable concept of the job they are applying for and why they want to make a change. I ask them what contributions they made to their organization, things they are most proud of. Then I ask about their frustrations and disappointments.

I ask if they have any questions to ask of me. This gives me further indication of their interest and how well the candidates have done their homework.

When I am interviewing a stockbroker candidate, for instance, I will look for sales orientation. Demeanor and physical appearance are important because a stockbroker will have to deal with the public on an ongoing basis. If a candidate has a sloppy appearance, he or she had better overwhelm me with some other qualities at our first meeting. It's also important that a candidate not slaughter the king's English.

In the initial conversation, one thing I try to find out is if a candidate will really fit into this corporate environment. For example, if you find a person who likes structure and black-and-white answers, he will not like it here. Nor will a person who likes a nice, peaceful, quiet environment. These things give me a reasonably quick indication that it will not be a good match.

At our firm we train our own people after they are hired, at a cost of several thousand dollars, which points out why short-term employments are red flags. After a person is trained and proved productive, someone outside is always willing to pay more. Another employer will get a trained employee he didn't have to pay to train, so he can offer a higher salary.

The benefit to the employee is a quick buck, but there are a lot of intangibles he or she loses out on. This is where people have to assess painstakingly what they are looking for in their careers and the choices they make.

An astute interviewer will not accept "The job wasn't all it was cracked up to be" as a viable excuse more than once. What the interviewer sees is that you did not take time to investigate the job thoroughly before you jumped at the money bait. This denotes poor decision-making, especially when there is a pattern of this type of activity.

Job candidates at our firm go through several tests and interviews before the final interview, which can run two or three hours.

I tell college students that if an employer says, "You're hired" after a half-hour interview, be wary. Even in a fast-food world, do not accept fast job offers without question. Insist on getting your questions answered. Or at least know what you're getting into. If it's a sink-or-swim situation, know it in advance.

I don't like game-playing in the hiring process. If I like your resume and call you in for an interview, it's a two-way street. We are both doing a selling job on one another in a sense, and we owe one another mutual respect and courtesy.

You are not a second-class citizen because you want to change a job, want a better job, or happen to be out of a job. I want people who are as interested in learning about the career opportunities we have to offer as I am to learn about what they have to offer.

[Hiring] is like creating a good marriage. It involves the melding of minds. You have to know that what I have to offer is going to match your needs, and vice versa.

If each of us takes the time to find out everything we need to know, we'll make a better decision. And the chances of sticking with that commitment are going to be much greater.

SOCIAL SECURITY

Employers are required to give you a form showing the amount of earnings that count for social security. They do this at the end of the year (or when you stop working for them if it is before the end of the year). These receipts (usually a W-2 form "Wage and Tax Statement") will help you should there be an error in the amount of earnings reported on the social security record.

The Social Security Administration has a special lifetime earnings record for you at its headquarters in Baltimore, Maryland. This record is available to you at any time, and will be sent at no charge, merely by filling out the card shown on the following page (available at your social security office for the asking).

It is prudent to request this every three years or so to make certain the social security taxes you are paying are being properly credited to your social security account. Recent errors are easier to correct. In some instances, an error cannot be corrected after approximately three years; the record stands.

SOCIAL SECURITY ADMINISTRATION

Request for Earnings and Benefit Estimate Statement

To receive a free statement of your earnings covered by Social Security and your estimated future benefits, all you need to do is fill out this form. Please print or type your answers. When you have completed the form, fold it and mail it to us.

1. Name shown on your Social Security card:

   First _____ Middle Initial _____ Last _____

2. Your Social Security number as shown on your card:

   ☐☐☐ - ☐☐ - ☐☐☐☐

3. Your date of birth:

   Month _____ Day _____ Year _____

4. Other Social Security numbers you may have used:

   ☐☐☐ - ☐☐ - ☐☐☐☐
   ☐☐☐ - ☐☐ - ☐☐☐☐

5. Your Sex: ☐ Male ☐ Female

6. Other names you have used (including a maiden name):

   _____

7. Show your actual earnings for last year and your estimated earnings for this year. Include only wages and/or net self-employment income subject to Social Security tax.

   A. Last year's actual earnings:

   $ ☐☐☐ , ☐☐☐ . ☐ ☐
   Dollars only

   B. This year's estimated earnings:

   $ ☐☐☐ , ☐☐☐ . ☐ ☐
   Dollars only

8. Show the age at which you plan to retire: _____

9. Below, show an amount which you think best represents your future average yearly earnings between now and when you plan to retire. The amount should be a yearly average, not your total future lifetime earnings. Only show earnings subject to Social Security tax.

   Most people should enter the same amount as this year's estimated earnings (the amount shown in 7B). The reason for this is that we will show your retirement benefit estimate in today's dollars, but adjusted to account for average wage growth in the national economy.

   However, if you expect to earn significantly more or less in the future than what you currently earn because of promotions, a job change, part-time work, or an absence from the work force, enter the amount in today's dollars that will most closely reflect your future average yearly earnings. Do not add in cost-of-living, performance, or scheduled pay increases or bonuses.

   Your future average yearly earnings:

   $ ☐☐☐ , ☐☐☐ . ☐ ☐
   Dollars only

10. Address where you want us to send the statement:

    Name _____

    Street Address (Include Apt. No., P.O. Box, or Rural Route) _____

    City _____ State _____ Zip Code _____

I am asking for information about my own Social Security record or the record of a person I am authorized to represent. I understand that if I deliberately request information under false pretenses I may be guilty of a federal crime and could be fined and/or imprisoned. I authorize you to send the statement of my earnings and benefit estimates to me or my representative through a contractor.

▶ Please sign your name (Do not print)

_____

Date _____ (Area Code) Daytime Telephone No. _____

ABOUT THE PRIVACY ACT

Social Security is allowed to collect the facts on this form under Section 205 of the Social Security Act. We need them to quickly identify your record and prepare the earnings statement you asked us for. Giving us these facts is voluntary. However, without them we may not be able to give you an earnings and benefit estimate statement. Neither the Social Security Administration nor its contractor will use the information for any other purpose.

Form SSA-7004-PC-OP3 (6/88) DESTROY PRIOR EDITIONS

☐ SP

Part 2

Sample Resumes

HOW TO USE
THE SAMPLE RESUMES

The sample resumes cover practically every employment category and job application, and were prepared by a professional resume firm that keeps abreast of employment trends and practices. The form, theory, and philosophy in these resumes represent employer thinking nationwide. The resume format offered is accepted as the standard, approved format for clarity of presentation and effectiveness of design.

If you cannot find the exact position for which you are applying, refer to the resume index at the front of the book. Look for the job titles that are closest. After locating the model that most closely parallels your own situation, use it as a model to structure your own resume.

Read all the resumes that in some way relate to your particular background or job objective. This will enable you to choose valuable ideas that may be neatly incorporated into your own resume. A variety of styles have been provided to aid in the creation of your resume. Select the style that you consider the most attractive, or combine styles to create a resume that is uniquely yours.

Note the editor's comments at the bottom of some resumes. They show how various problem areas are treated and can help your resume preparation should your career background not fit into any standard mold.

Synopsis of Resume:

STEWART T. MORRIS

62 Crestview Park • Rogers City, MI 49779 • (517) 813-8903

Job Objective:	Educational Administration

Experience:

1989–Present	**Superintendent of Schools** Rogers City, MI
1987–89	**Supervising Principal** Board of Education, Sheboygan, MI
1977–87	**Director of Physical Education** Board of Education, Gaylord, MI

Education:

1972–76	**University of Michigan**, Ann Arbor, MI (Completed five-year course in four years)

Degrees:	B.S. in Physical Education B.A. (cum laude)—Science minor M.S. in Education (1985)
Activities:	Varsity basketball; all intramural sports; received annual cup for all-around athletic achievement; social fraternity president, senior year.
Note:	Total of 20 hours beyond master's degree, acquired as time and location have permitted. Expect to continue on same basis.

Interests:	Sports (active and spectator); music appreciation; fitness
Affiliations:	Rotary International; Michigan State Teachers' Association; Michigan State City and Village Superintendents; active in local affairs—see following for complete listing.

Willing to relocate.

(FOR AMPLIFICATION, SEE FOLLOWING.)

Stresses success in handling people, as well as esteem in which applicant is held, as indicated by elected office and membership in responsible organizations; record merits three pages.

Amplified Resume:

Employment Highlights

1989–Present
Superintendent of Schools

Employed as a Superintendent of a system composed of a senior high, a junior high, and four elementary schools.

Directed school system centralization with outgoing districts. Bus routes have been put into operation; approximately $18,000,000 in new buildings have been added (three complete buildings plus other additions); four bond issues have been proposed to and passed by the community.

Faculty has grown from 85 to 120; student body has increased from 1,500 to 2,700. Scholarship has been maintained at a high level. Pupil achievement averages are in top percentile of country; scholarships earned by students in system have risen to 16 of the 25 offered to all the systems in country. Employee turnover remarkably low—losses to other systems almost nil. In public relations area, have successfully accomplished difficult task of pleasing public, faculty, and students during constant change and multitudinous school money problems.

Responsibilities include: (1) preparation, presentation, and enforcement of budgets; (2) finding and hiring qualified teachers; (3) curriculum in system; (4) contact with and follow-up on architectural planning and construction of all buildings, plus specifying and installing all new equipment; (5) personnel supervisor.

Reason for desiring change: Desire to leave public life.

1987–89
Supervising Principal

As Supervising Principal was confronted with task of taking school through complex centralized procedures.

Spoke to groups of citizens at all levels; successfully solved the multiple problems that arose. Supervised planning and construction of new centralized building, as well as its ultimate operation and operating personnel.

Reason for leaving: To accept position above.

(Continued)

Stewart T. Morris
-Page 3-

1977–87
Director of Physical Education

Coached all athletic teams; planned all gymnasium programs. Success indicated by record of winning teams (several championships in basketball and football), in addition to outstanding record of cooperation from both students and other faculty members. Completed Master's in Education during this period; left to take supervisory position.

General

Positions held:

1. President of Central Zone of Michigan State Teachers' Association (10,000 teachers).

2. State Director, Michigan State Teachers' Association.

3. Chairman, Michigan State Fund-Raising Drive for Retired Teachers' Home.

4. Past Chairman, Michigan State Teachers' Public Relations Committee.

5. Past President, Rogers City Rotary Club.

6. Board of Directors of: Rogers City Savings Bank, Michigan State Public High School Athletic Association, Michigan State Public High School Athletic Protection Plan (insurance).

7. Chairman: Christmas and Easter Seal Drive, annual Red Cross Drive, Civic Music Association Drive.

8. Member, Executive Committee, Michigan State High School Athletic Association.

References available.

Synopsis of Resume:

MICHAEL PETRAKOS

---

300 Rosemoor Drive • **Chicago, IL 60648** • **312-497-8745**

JOB OBJECTIVE: Position in the field of Industrial Relations, utilizing personnel, science, industrial, engineering, and accounting background

EXPERIENCE:
1988–Present
Personnel Director: Apex Camera Company
Photo Products Division, Chicago, IL
Progressed through Tabulating Research, Industrial Engineering, and Inventory Control positions into managerial position.

1986–88
Management Trainee
United Life Insurance Co., New York, NY
Two-year program.
Left on completion; wished to change fields.

1983–86
General Office Work
Harrison Electric Products, Louisville, KY
Offered managerial training during and after college period.
Resigned to accept position above.

EDUCATION:
1979–83
University of Louisville, Louisville, KY
Degrees: B.S. in Business Administration
B.S. in Chemistry
Honors: Offered fellowship for graduate study;
finances prevented acceptance.

Continuing Education:
Industrial Engineering; MTM (Methods, Time, Measurement) Conference; seminars on Leadership, Human Relations, and Work Measurement

INTERESTS: Sailing; golf; bridge

AFFILIATIONS: Industrial Management Council

Will relocate for the proper opportunity.

(FOR AMPLIFICATION, SEE FOLLOWING.)

*One major employment record, showing chronology of promotions as well as
increased level of responsibility through increased number of personnel involved.*

Amplified Resume:

EMPLOYMENT HIGHLIGHTS

1988–Present
Apex Camera Co.

1992   Moved to Photo Products Division and was promoted to department head of inventory control. Supervised six separate offices with 120 personnel, whose function was preparation of payroll, production control, and in-process inventory records.

     Restored order to a department that was disorganized due to transfer of previous department head. Streamlined operations; handled increased work load from production increase with same work force; boosted morale.

     At request of Division Superintendent, prepared special cost analysis of old payroll reporting methods compared with cost of computer applications. Developed presentation which reached top-level management.

     Promoted to present position of Personnel Director of Photo Products Division, with over 2,500 personnel. Personally interview and coordinate hiring of business and engineering personnel. Screen records, recommend promotions, make decisions on upgrading.

1990   Industrial Engineering Department. Assignments included office systems and methods, plant layout, production methods, and cost studies. Assignments based on accounting background included:

     1. System of company gross profit shrinkage. **Result:** substantial reduction of loss by proper accounting methods, with major reduction in paperwork.

     2. Efficiency study of cafeteria operations to mimimize annual six-figure loss. **Result:** major reduction of loss to manageable level.

     3. Coordinating and directing the relocation of Industrial Engineering Dept. Involved working with construction engineers, planning and timing move sequences so as to eliminate work interruption. Completed precisely on schedule.

1988   Employed in Tabulating Research Department; assigned to development of computer systems for payroll and production.

References available.

Synopsis of Resume:

ALAN L. THOMASON
30 Sutton Street
Hattiesburg, MS 39401
(601) 761-4132

OBJECTIVE: Position in field of Personnel, College Recruitment, or College Relations

EXPERIENCE:

October 1989–
Present

Director of Placement and Alumni Relations
Assistant Director of Admissions
Mississippi Southern College, Hattiesburg, MS

1988–89

Purchasing Agent
Randolph Chemical Co., Butler, AL
Resigned to accept the position above.

1985–88

Red Cross Swimming Instructor
Summers and part-time during college years.

EDUCATION:

1984–88

University of Arkansas

Degree:	B.S. in Social Sciences
Honors:	Dean's list four times
Expenses:	Financed 75% of college expenses.
Activities:	President of: Junior and Senior classes, Student Board of Governors, Inter-College Council of American Red Cross. Member of Glee Club and Debating Team.

1980–84

Allendale Preparatory School, Lake Charles, LA
Valedictorian of class; awarded year's scholarship for
European study and travel.

INTERESTS: Swimming; sailing; stamp collecting

AFFILIATIONS: Southern College Personnel Officers' Association
Mississippi State Deans & Guidance Counselors' Association
Mississippi State Counselors' Association

Free to relocate.

(FOR AMPLIFICATION, SEE FOLLOWING.)

*Although shooting for industry, stresses extraordinary
accomplishments in present position, demonstrating the energy
and initiative obviously usable and desirable in any field.*

Amplified Resume:

Alan L. Thomason
-Page 2-

EMPLOYMENT HIGHLIGHTS

10/89–Present
Mississippi Southern College

Originally employed as Assistant Director of Placement and Admissions.
Promoted to present classification after one year.

As Director of Placement, responsible for senior and alumni placement,
teacher placement, and part-time or summer positions for undergraduates.
Advise students and perform employment evaluations.

As Assistant Director of Admissions, set up a system of recruitment for the
college. Gave talks before high school students and various interest groups in Mississippi
Southern College. Later, passed on qualifications of applicants.

In placement field have made extensive contacts with desirable companies; have increased
number of companies interviewing students from 75 to 120. Further this interest by speaking
before various civic organizations. Keep posted on requirements for a variety of
fields and positions, then steer interviewers to right prospects. Entire program
has been highly successful; relations with students and industry, excellent.

In newly created position of Director of Alumni Relations, inaugurate a policy of
regular contact; serve as a liaison between alumni, faculty, and students.

Positive Results:

1. Dues-paying alumni percentage increased from 11% to 39%. National average
   is approximately 19%.

2. Participation in insurance program benefiting college increased from 20 % to 35%.

3. Initiated a systematic contribution program supplementing the above.

General:

1. Serve as Chairperson of Committee in Scholarship.

2. Coordinate Graduate School studies; advise on financial aid available.

Reason for desiring change: Seeking income commensurate with experience and ability.

References available.

GRACE OSBORNE
5010 Sun Circle
Colorado Springs, CO 80907
(303) 457-4820

Objective: Fund-raising

Experience:

1989–Present   **Fund-raising Chairperson**
Democratic Campaign Headquarters
General Election

1986–89   **Director of Development**
Colorado College, Colorado Springs, CO

1973–75   **Director of Development**
St. Mary's School for the Deaf, Buffalo, NY

1970–73   **Coordinator, Curriculum Development Center**
State University of New York at Buffalo, Buffalo, NY

Volunteer Service:

1983–Present   **Democratic Executive Committee**
Precinct Captain, Steering Committee; State Convention
Delegate; Vice-Chairperson, Political Action Committee

1976–82   **League of Women Voters**
Board of Directors; Human Resources Chairperson; Project
Director of Statewide Education Fund Conference;
Coordinator for Equal Rights Amendment Ratification

Education:

1969   **Merril-Palmer Institute,** Detroit, MI
Graduate Study in Early Childhood Education

1964–68   **University of North Carolina,** Greensboro, NC
Degree: B.A. Sociology

Free to travel but not to relocate. References available on request.

*One page serves purpose here. Impressive background creates enough interest
to generate interview where details can be discussed.*

PAUL H. CARPENTER

---

148 Palmer Avenue • Des Moines, IA 50315 • (515) 631-0551

JOB OBJECTIVE: Position as Insurance Specialist (Casualty, Fire, Marine) for banking real estate department, or position where extensive management experience can be fully utilized.

EXPERIENCE:

1980–92   **Manager**
Des Moines Casualty Insurance Co., Des Moines, IA

Employed as an underwriter. Approved or rejected business written for all forms of casualty insurance. Required expert knowledge of property evaluations and ability to judge past performance of individuals and justify decision to salesperson and property owner if rejected. In four years promoted to Assistant Manager. In 1983 promoted to Manager. Duties similar, with more responsibility inherent to Manager's spot.

Directed approximately 35 full-time employees; supervised efforts of 125 agents. Continuously recruited, encouraged, trained and worked with new personnel. Worked with agents through approximately six special agents in the office; was final authority on problems which persisted. Hired and trained office, clerical, and accounting personnel. Supervised prompt processing of applications and policies and collection of delinquencies, and handled claims from insureds.

During term as manager, company went through reorganization and top management change. Company policy dictated drastic cutbacks and economies in all offices, plus a change in representation policies. As a direct result of the latter, Des Moines office lost agencies taking with them a substantial six-figure volume in premiums.

Record during management period
More than regained the loss above; have increased the dollar volume. Properly and promptly handled the increased volume, plus paperwork resulting from agency changes, with force of 15 (reduced from 30). Expanded full company services to the large area surrounding Des Moines, whereas only fire had been offered previously outside Polk County.

Reason for resignation: Impending transfer to undesirable location.

(Continued)

1970–80   **Partner**
Empire Insurance Agency, Des Moines, IA

Formed company with partner. Acted as underwriter and office manager.
Company dissolved when partner was forced to withdraw for health reasons.

Underwriter
Bismark Casualty and Surety Co., Bismark, ND

1970   Transferred to Des Moines, Iowa, with larger responsibility. Because
of record, was invited by superior to join him in forming the above company.
Resigned to do so.

1968–70   Employed as clerk trainee; promoted to underwriter. Received extensive company
training and joined self-training program.

EDUCATION: High school graduate; Underwriters Board courses in various phases
of insurance; numerous company courses in casualty, marine, and
general insurance

AFFILIATIONS: Rotary Club; Chamber of Commerce

Will relocate for exceptional opportunity.

References available on request.

*Synopsis page avoided in record of older person where last or present employment
has been of considerable duration. Immediate employment amplification serves to put
immediate focus on most significant aspect of record—namely, experience.*

Synopsis of Resume:

LISA M. CARLUCCI
3340 Brookemeade Drive
Seattle, WA 98122
(206) 632-7012

Job Objective: Program Specialist in private sector

Experience:
1990–Present   **Program Specialist**
                            Seattle Central Community College, Seattle, WA

1982–90   **Assistant Director of Admissions**
                            Lowell School of Design, New York, NY

1980–82   **Secondary School Art Teacher**
                            Ludlow Junior High School, Ludlow, MA

1976–80   **Elementary School Art Teacher**
                            Warwick Public Schools, Warwick, RI

Other: Part-time work to help defray cost of education: arts and crafts
                            camp counselor; freelance artist; retail sales

Education:
1970–76   **Rhode Island School of Design,** Providence, RI
                            Degree: B.F.A. in Graphic Arts Design

Other: Miscellaneous ongoing computer courses

Interests: Painting; classical piano; reading

(FOR AMPLIFICATION, SEE FOLLOWING.)

Amplified Resume:

Lisa M. Carlucci
-Page 2-

Employment Highlights

1990–Present
Seattle Central Community College
Enrollment 10,000

As Program Specialist for the Center of Continuing Education and Community Center, general responsibilities encompass assisting with the developing and marketing of non-credit programming.

Write copy and design graphics for brochures and direct mail-outs; plan publicity and coordinate advertising and photo assignments; supervise photo production.

Specific responsibilities include interviewing prospective teachers, developing courses, acting as audiovisual coordinator, and organizing seminars and special events.

Reason for desiring change: Interest in obtaining private-sector position with potential to fully utilize diverse skills and experience.

1982–90
Lowell School of Design

As Assistant Director of Admissions, conduct local and out-of-state recruitment. Interview prospective students; evaluate artistic abilities and admission credentials. Act as Director of Admissions in Director's absence. Hire, train, and supervise staff of student aides. During tenure, applications rose over 50%, enrollment 30%. Salary increased significantly.

1976–82
Art Teacher

Art teaching assignments in both elementary and secondary school capacities, involving classroom teaching, developing art curricula, establishing departmental budgets, and setting up professional workshops.

References on request

Synopsis of Resume:

GEOFFREY L. PFEFFER
87 Puritan Road
Somerville, MA 02145
(617) 988-5682

EXPERIENCE:

1988–Present   **Regional Director**
                      NewComp, Inc., Boston, MA
                      ($200 million in volume)

1974–88   **Systems Analyst Officer**
                      Bank of Boston, Boston, MA

EDUCATION:

1967–74   **Stonehill College,** North Easton, MA
                      Degree: B.A.   **Major:** Economics

                      American Institute of Banking
                      Seminars: Effective Communication; Effective Analysis;
                      Effective Management; database concepts; programming
                      classes including IBM Cobol and Assembler

INTERESTS: Chess; theater; reading; bridge; racquetball

AFFILIATIONS: Association for Systems Management; Country Playhouse;
                      Community Chest; church-affiliated Mens' Service Club

                      Salary negotiable • Will relocate for right opportunity

(FOR AMPLIFICATION, SEE FOLLOWING.)

*At this level, "Job Objective" need not be shown, giving latitude
to submit record as opportunities in field surface.*

Amplified Resume:

Geoffrey L. Pfeffer
-Page 2-

EMPLOYMENT HIGHLIGHTS

1988 - Present
    NewComp, Inc.
    Employs 6,000 nationally; 2,500 locally

    Initially acted as Assistant Manager of team consisting of two to ten persons; supervised detailed functional and design phases of a deposit product.

    Promoted to present position of Regional Director with salary raise to high five figures. Manage group of four business analysts who design and execute a test system for an integrated bank system and who advise corporation on banking situations. Achieve marked success in CIF (Central Information File) and CD (Certificate of Deposit) products.

    Reason for change: Desire greater responsibility and challenge.

1974 - 1988
    Bank of Boston
    17th-largest assets in U.S.

    Programmer Trainee, promoted to Systems Officer making recommendations to every department in bank. Work on eight projects simultaneously, including automation of wire-room services; improve work flow in proof and transit and cost justification on new computer system.

    Reason for leaving: To accept position with NewComp, Inc.

References available in confidence following interview.

Synopsis of Resume:

DAVID L. SHAPIRO

---

47 Beecher Place　•　Bangor, ME 04401　•　(207) 822-9177

OBJECTIVE: Position as artist, designer, or creative writer for advertising or promotion work. Industrial advertising or agency.

EXPERIENCE:

1989–92 　　**Mechanical Paste-Up in Design —Art Department**
Langie Paper Container Corp., Bangor, ME

1987–89　　**Advertising Manager**
Jewett Department Store, Third Street, Bangor, ME

1985–87　　**Freelance Designer**
Augusta, ME

1983–85　　**Chief of Jewelry Design**
Best Arts, Inc., Tremont Blvd., Bangor, ME

1981–83　　**Poster Designer & Rubber Plate Engraver**
Porter Wells Inc., Prince Street, Boston, MA

Prior:　　**Assistant Window Trimmer**
　　Beck's Department Store, Salem MA
Layout, Design, Copywriting
　　Makin Advertising Agency, Salem, MA
Home Photography
　　Freer Photographers, Salem, MA

— Left each job to accept improved position.

EDUCATION:

1976–79　　**Maryland Institute College of Art,** Baltimore, MD
　　Courses included: Advertising Design, Photography,
　　Interior Decorating, Illustration, Life Drawing

INTERESTS: Painting; camping; fishing

AFFILIATIONS: Board member of the Bangor Memorial Art Gallery

(FOR AMPLIFICATION, SEE FOLLOWING.)

This is a field in which pictures and samples are literally more significant than a thousand resume words. Therefore, resume merely points out training and experience indicating, wherever possible, samples of work available for review. To enclose or attach such samples could restrict opportunity to be invited for an interview.

Amplified Resume:

David L. Shapiro
-Page 2-

EMPLOYMENT HIGHLIGHTS

1989–92
Langie Paper Container Corporation
Manufacturers of cartons and packing containers
Designer/Artist. Assist in package design and perform mechanical paste-up
of designs for packages, boxes, or cartons, primarily of food container type. Lost
position when business filed for bankruptcy.

1987–89
Jewett Department Store
Clothing retailer
Advertising Manager. Prepare copy and artwork. Design layouts
for news media, selecting material of reader interest and slanting it to
acceptable style and store policy. Create and arrange store and window displays.
Photographs of such displays and samples of newspaper ads available for
inspection. Resigned to accept position above, which appeared to hold greater
potential.

1985–87
Freelance
Obtain commissions through personal initiative (restaurant murals, portraits, etc.)
Assist established designers. Write and photograph several articles on fishing
and outdoor life; seven nationally published articles available for review.

1983–85
Best Arts, Inc.
School and organizational jewelry
Jewelry Design Manager. Work from written description or rough sketch of desired
article. Make and submit accurate formal drawing of item to school or organization for
approval. Upon acceptance, forward drawing to metal-die department for duplication.
Samples of work available. Resigned to do freelance work.

1981–83
Porter Wells, Inc.
Poster art
Trainee. Learn rubber plate engraving for reproduction of posters.
Make pencil drawings on tracing paper, which are rubbed down into rubber
plates to become guides for hand cutting with engraving tools. Progress
into original creative poster design. Resigned to gain additional experience
in other art fields.

References and samples available on request.

Synopsis of Resume:

LINDA KURTZ
155 Oakville Avenue
Rye, New York 10580
(716) 555-9862

JOB OBJECTIVE:	Fashion Coordinator
EXPERIENCE:	
1985–Present	**Fashion Coordinator** Hentley Department Store, New York, NY
1984–85	**Co-owner, Bridal Shop** Sakowitz, Houston, TX
1982–84	**Model and Teacher** Kentall Modeling School, Pittsburgh, PA
1980–82	**Weather Reporter, Television Commercials** WJZ-TV, Baltimore, MD
Prior:	Freelance modeling—London, Paris
EDUCATION:	

1974–78	**Northwestern University**
	    Major: Advertising (Business Administration)
	    Minor: Applied Arts

LANGUAGES:	Fluent in French; working knowledge of Spanish
INTERESTS:	Water sports; sculpting (clay, metal); pottery; fashion research
AFFILIATIONS:	Art League; Red Flat Charette (environmental organization)

(FOR AMPLIFICATION, SEE FOLLOWING.)

Heavy experience divided into major categories of fashion interest to prevent its being clouded in the sea of detail inherent in the work of fashion consulting.

Amplified Resume:

Linda Kurtz
-Page 2-

EMPLOYMENT HIGHLIGHTS

1985–Present
Hentley Department Store

Employed as Fashion Coordinator for leading New York City department store, with responsibilities centered in four major areas: fashion, display, training, and public relations.

Fashion—Full responsibility for eight to ten major fashion shows a year, plus smaller in-store shows, and shows organized for various community organization functions.

Hire models, select clothes appropriate to season or theme, and meet with buyers and display personnel to communicate needs for lighting, decorating, music, and amplification. Supervise rehearsals and deliver commentary on day of show. At show conclusion, write models' vouchers, check merchandise return to store, and evaluate gains made in increased sales.

Display—Responsible for "Front and Forward," a program devised to create a unified look for the store by coordinating all displays, cases, and T-stands.

Training—On own initiative, set up training program for all ready-to-wear sales personnel. Hold daily departmental meetings to familiarize salespersons with featured advertised merchandise in daily papers and to point out unique selling points of stock. Hold bimonthly fashion meetings with focus on total store fashion message and inventory.

Public Relations—Organize and implement store's seasonal holiday breakfasts and brunches given periodically throughout the year for general public.

Responsible for store's annual Sewing Contest. Follow entries through to final judging. Give commentary and present final awards. Write publicity releases; accept public speaking engagements at women's clubs; make occasional radio and television appearances.

Reason for desiring change: To obtain position commensurate with experience and ability.

References on request. Please do not contact present employer at this time.

KIMBERLY MAIER
3762 North Florida Avenue
Lakeland, Florida 33805
(813) 356-4554

OBJECTIVE: Television Commercials; Modeling; Dinner Theater

DESCRIPTION: Actress, Singer, Dancer, Model

Height:	5'6"
Weight:	108
Eyes:	Green
Hair:	Chestnut

EXPERIENCE:

T.V. / Radio   **National:**
New Weight Diet Wafer (solo commercial); Lovely Panty Hose;
Pro Tennis Shoes

Local:
Tim Kantor Show (one-woman Gershwin show); Jeff Arthur Productions
(jingles); Jacques Brel (filmed for T.V. as live theater); radio and T.V. commercials

Theater   Champlain Valley Shakespeare Festival, Burlington, VT
     As You Like It; The Tempest
Goodman Repertory Company; Chicago, IL
     Heartbreak House, Dutchman
Royal Tyler Theatre, Burlington, VT
     The Man Who Came to Dinner, Three Sisters; Born Yesterday;
     Cat on a Hot Tin Roof; The Death of Bessie Smith
Monomoy Summer Theater, Cape Cod, MA
     Cabaret; Sabrina; The Skin of Our Teeth; Charley's Aunt
St. Mark's Place Theatre Ensemble, NYC
     The Contrast; Sweet Bird of Youth
TGL Theatre, Burlington, VT
     Writer and choreographer of original Gershwin Revue

(Continued)

Club Performances: Bottom Line Cabaret Theatre; Blue Garter Cabaret; Knickerbocker Saloon; The Blue Note (New York City); Big Band lead vocals with Casey & Company, New England Tour (songs of the thirties and the forties)

One-woman musicals for various local clubs and organizations

EDUCATION: **Oberlin Conservatory of Music**
Concentration in Drama
University of South Florida
Master's in Theater

Studied dance under Holby Grethe, New York City
Studied acting under Jerry Roth, Burlington, VT

ADDITIONAL SKILLS: Artist; lyricist; pianist; jingle writer; copywriter

Free to travel or relocate anywhere in the U.S., Canada, or Mexico

Synopsis of Resume:

SUSAN WAYNE

3978 Sandridge Drive • Atlanta, GA 30305 • (414) 233-0875

Objective:	Position in communications that would utilize educational major and current experience
Experience:	
1990–Present	**Assistant Traffic Director**
	Camera Assistant
	WEAT-TV, Atlanta, GA
Part Time:	
1988–90	**Classroom Aide** (Headstart program)
	Sarasota Board of Education, Sarasota, FL
	Sales, window dressing, modeling
	Maas Department Store, Sarasota, FL
Education:	
1984–88	**Florida State University**
	Degree: Bachelor of Arts
	Major: Mass Communications
Interests:	Amateur theater; tennis; water sports
Affiliations:	YMCA; Community Theater; Civic Museum Association

(FOR AMPLIFICATION, SEE FOLLOWING.)

*Anxious to get foot in the door of larger-market television studio; consequently
avoided specific objective that would narrow opportunity for being considered
for any possible opening.*

Amplified Resume:

Susan Wayne
-Page 2-

Employment Highlights

July 1990–Present
WEAT–TV, Atlanta, GA

Promoted to Traffic Director after working four months as general clerk. Duties involve creating a television log; procuring sales availabilities for sales department; organizing and preparing billing information for bookkeeping department; pulling and distributing teletype data; contacting syndicators and distributors of taped shows and films to insure proper scheduling and playdates; and preparing advance program information for television publications.

Organize film department upon resignation of film director. Train film director's replacement in innovative film handling and shipping procedures, resulting in streamlined film department.

Assist in production of commercials. Appear on camera for several taped commercials. Operate camera on both live and taped local shows. Write copy and read voice-overs.

Reason for leaving: Wish to relocate to larger market area.

References available on request.

GLORIA MORALES

865 Bannaker Way #5 • Montgomery, AL 36195 • (205) 366-7652

Objective: General Assignment Reporter or Area Correspondent

Experience:

1990–Present **Reporter**
Montgomery Press, Montgomery, AL
(Circulation: 50,000)

1988–90 **Assistant Editor**
Covington Herald, Covington, LA
(Circulation 14,000)

Other: Editor of high school and college newspapers

Education:

1987 **University of Alabama,** Tuscaloosa, AL
Degree: B.A. in Journalism
Minor: Political Science
Honors: Deans' List; Editor of newspaper

Special Skills: Word processing; desktop publishing; 25mm and 120 Rolex; photo sizing and cropping; paste-up; proofing; editing; headlines

Interests: Tennis; swimming; reading; writing

Employment Highlights: **Montgomery Press:** General assignment reporter covering hard news, including City Council, school boards, and various community interest meetings. Interview personalities/celebrities on special photo/journal assignments. Cover for entertainment editor on occasion.

Covington Herald: Assistant Editor for small weekly newspaper. Ensured all deadlines were met. Word processed articles and designed newspaper. Wrote general news items as time permitted. Resigned to accept above position.

Free to relocate
Portfolio and references available upon request

Combining both synopsis and employment detail on a one-page resume that adequately serves in view of short record, pointing up nonetheless a variety of specific, usable skills.

Synopsis of Resume:

MICHAEL SIMMONS
6440 Oregon Street
Fort Meyers, FL 33901
(813) 297 - 5590

JOB OBJECTIVE: Production Manager

EXPERIENCE:

1989–Present   **Production Manager**
                      WXLF-TV, Fort Meyers, FL

1987–89   **Production Manager**
                      WAEO, Rhinelander, WI

1983–86   **Chief, Information Division**
                      United States Army

Part-time/
Summer jobs: Freelance copywriter for advertising firms;
                      Radiographer, Pipeweld X-Ray Corp.

EDUCATION:

1978–82   **Syracuse University,** Syracuse, NY
                      Degree: B.S. in Broadcasting

Other: **Northeast Broadcasting School,** Boston, MA

INTERESTS: Writing; music; woodworking; golf

AFFILIATIONS: Writer's Club; Palmaire Golf Club

(FOR AMPLIFICATION, SEE FOLLOWING.)

Amplified Resume:

Michael Simmons
-Page 2-

EMPLOYMENT HIGHLIGHTS

June 1989–Present
WXLF-TV, Ft. Myers, FL

Production Manager of new television station. Responsible for initial airdate preparation and in full charge of all production following airdate, including newscasts, commercial announcements, programs, and administrative details. Due to small staff, carry additional responsibilities of program director, continuity writer, staff announcer, and camera assistant. Station holds national network rating well beyond expectation for a new station in a comparable time period.

Reason for desiring change: Wish to concentrate in production area of larger, established station.

January 1987–June 1989
WAEO, Rhinelander, WI

Continuity writer; promoted in two months to Production Director. Responsible for all commercial production and attendant details.

Reason for leaving: Amicable separation to accept present position.

1983–86
United States Army

Chief, Information Division. Write, narrate, film, and direct half-hour color documentary. Provide news releases; film and supply news film to national news services. Solely responsible for any news released.

Reason for leaving: Honorable discharge.

References on request

Synopsis of Resume:

Patricia Keegan
9972 Lone Tree
Dallas, TX 75218
(214) 382 - 4391

Objective: Public Affairs Director

Experience:

1990–Present   **Public Affairs Director;**
                        Talk Show Hostess; Reporter
                        WXTN-TV, Dallas, Texas

1987–90   **Traffic and Continuity Coordinator**
                        WYND, Slidell, Louisiana

1985–87   **Production Assistant**
                        WQED-TV, Houston, Texas

1982–85   **Continuity and Production Assistant**
                        WVIZ, Cleveland, Ohio

Education:

1978–82   **Ohio State University**
                        Major: Journalism
                        Minor: Communications media

Other: **New York University**
                            Summer workshop in radio and television
                        Dallas Advertising Club
                            Public relations seminar

Languages: Spanish (fluent), French (working knowledge)

Interests: Swimming; scuba; sewing; puppetry; art; painting

Affiliations: Dallas Press Club; Museum Director; Ecology Committee;
                        Professional Women's Club

(FOR AMPLIFICATION, SEE FOLLOWING.)

*Despite frequent job changes, progression in salary and responsibilities
form a logical sequence. Emphasis on affiliations strengthens
qualifications for objective.*

Amplified Resume:

Employment Highlights

1990–Present
WXTN-TV, Dallas, TX

News reporter. Cover civic and cultural events, politics, and news features. Shoot, process, and edit film; write and produce audio commentary.

Talk show hostess. Responsible for hour-long live broadcast aired daily by station as a public relations project. Design set, create opening and close, procure clothing sponsor to furnish daily wardrobe. Schedule and brief guests, including U.S. senators, actors, celebrities, and concerned citizens within broadcast range.

Public Affairs Director. Responsible for above plus moderate panel discussions and special programs on various issues.

Reason for desiring change: Seeking salary commensurate with ability and experience.

1987–90
WYND, Slidell, LA

Traffic and continuity coordinator. Was responsible for daily log as well as continuity; wrote commercial copy and station promotional material; performed occasional on-air spots and voice-overs; filled in for talk show hostess when needed. Resigned to accept above position.

1985–87
WQED-TV (Educational), Houston, TX

Production assistant. Designed sets and graphics; served as liaison between the technical and instructional personnel. Resigned to accept above position.

1982–85
WVIZ, Cleveland, OH

Production assistant for city's new educational television station. Assisted traffic coordinator (daily logs and program guides). Amicable separation to accept position with more production emphasis.

References on request

Synopsis of Resume:

Yaphen Chang

33 Rand Place • Atlanta, GA 30315 • (404) 897 - 9641

Objective:	Field of Public Relations—Promotion—Advertising
Education: 1984–88	**Mt. Holyoke College**, South Hadley, MA **Degree:** A.B. **Major:** English Assistant Editor of college literary publication
Other:	"Experiment in International Living"—Competitive program selecting young Americans to represent U.S. in foreign countries. Selection on basis of scholastic achievement, physical fitness, personality, and character. Upon selection, spent six weeks with French family in 1982. Travel extensively; speak Chinese and French fluently.
Experience: 2/90–Present	**Promotion Writer** (With multiple additional responsibilities) KYKA-TV, 890 South Main Street, Atlanta, GA
10/88 - 11/89	**Office Assistant** Mather Advertising, Inc., Radio and TV Advertising 70 Stone Street, Boston, MA Secretarial and general office work
Interests:	Tennis; golf; music (accomplished pianist) **Willing to relocate anywhere in the U.S.**

(FOR AMPLIFICATION, SEE FOLLOWING.)

Field in which superior education is likely to carry more weight than average experience would; therefore, former is given synopsis page preference.

Amplified Resume:

Employment Highlights

1990–Present
KYKA-TV, Atlanta, GA

> Promotion writer responsible for all on-the-air promotion (30 sec.,
> 60 sec., etc.) for each day's log. Utilize organizational skills and
> creative writing ability to create spots and promotion on schedule.
> Responsible for all trailers, tapes, slides, and videotapes. Check and
> process them on arrival; screen for use. Determine what will be used,
> discarded, or cut; instruct film department on proper cutting procedure
> to attain desired length and content.

> Log all promotional announcements, check traffic boards, and maintain
> Kardex file. Fill out promotion orders, promotion reports, and program
> schedules; distribute to proper departments. Make periodic program checks
> to insure information is correct and current.

> **Reason for desiring change:** Desire position with more clearly defined
> responsibilities.

10/88–11/89
Mather Advertising, Inc., Boston, MA

> Secretarial and office work. Broadening responsibilities
> include radio and television copy and limited account servicing.
> Acquired introductory experience in packaging shows, public
> relations, and agency media work.

> **Reason for leaving:** To accept improved position.

References available

L. ROBERT BAUMAN

3897 Jay Street
Rochester, NY 14611
(716) 733 - 8120

JOB OBJECTIVE: Public Relations—Public Information

EXPERIENCE:

1988–Present

> **Monroe County Public Schools,** Rochester, NY
> Public Information Officer of county school system, working directly
> under Superintendent of Schools, who reports to the Board of Education.
>
> Liaison between School Board, various media, United Way, and the
> Disaster Preparedness Office.
>
> Duties encompass writing, editing, and coordinating graphics of four periodicals:
> (1) Quarterly newspaper—40,000 distribution
> (2) Monthly report on a specific school, together with activities and
>   pictures—4,000 distribution
> (3) Biweekly internal newsletter
> (4) Annual School Board Report—120,000 distribution
>
> Additional duties include writing, hosting, and producing a biweekly television
> program that spotlights personnel, activities, and achievements of individual
> students to increase parental and public awareness of local school system.
>
> Directly responsible for the management of the Public Information Office, which
> includes personnel, budget, printing, and distribution of periodicals.

(Continued)

L. Robert Bauman
-Page 2-

1973–88
Lee County Board of Instruction
Ft. Meyers, Florida

> Department supervisor, promoted from instrumental classroom
> music teacher upon selection as one of the "Outstanding
> Teachers in America." Co-author of "Elementary Music Curriculum
> Guide." Guest clinician at state-sponsored "Early Childhood and
> Elementary Education" conference.

1973–88 (Summers)

> Host two-hour classical music program over WZAY radio during July
> and August, five mornings a week.

EDUCATION:

1969–73

> **University State Teacher's College**
> **Crane Music School**, Potsdam, NY
> Degree: B.S. in Music Education

INTERESTS: Piano; singing

Willing to relocate

References available

Unusual field and qualifications do not lend themselves to synopsis
treatment as effectively as hitting the story head-on.

Synopsis of Resume:

FRANK L. PALMER

---

23 ANTLERS DRIVE • LAKE BLUFF, IL 60044 • (309) 629 - 5742

Objective:	Training position in Computer Programming where education in field can be utilized.
Experience:	
1990–Present	**Hydrometer Calibrator / Instrument Assembler** American Optical Co., Lake Bluff, IL
1986–90	**Dental Technician 1/C** U.S. Navy Honorable discharge; no reserve obligation
Prior:	Part-time and summer employment. Contribute significantly to family finances and defray full cost of college studies.
Education:	
1985	**Wichita Institute of Technology**, Wichita, KS Emphasis on college-level math; left voluntarily to enter the service.
1980–84	**Hayes High School**, Hates, KS Awarded scholarship to institute above
Other:	**Computer Center**, Lake Bluff, IL. Programming courses taken include COBAL, ALC, and FORTRAN. Operations courses include Introduction to E.D.P., Advanced Operating Systems, and RPG II.
Interests:	Sports; stamp collecting
Affiliations:	Men's Civic Club; Lion's Club

(FOR AMPLIFICATION, SEE FOLLOWING.)

Resume for trainee applicant stressing self-starting qualities, one of the most looked-for qualifications in trainees.

Amplified Resume:

Frank L. Palmer
-Page 2-

Employment Highlights

1990–Present
American Optical Company
Manufacturer of temperature and other precision instruments

Received promotion to hydrometer calibrator and merit increase of $6,000 after six months as instrument assembler. Perform duties unassisted. Beginning with bare instruments of various sizes, use several basic fluids at controlled temperatures. Use mathamatical interpolations to fit scales into tubes for proper reading with various solutions. Except for special rush and/or emergency orders, set own work pace. Operate glass tube and bulb machinery as necessary to produce own supplies and avoid backlog of orders.

Reason for desiring change: Wish to enter field of computer programming.

General

Entirely on own initiative, pursue continuing education in computer programming and data processing. Instruction includes actual operation of various machines, as well as programming experience. Marks range from "A" to "B+."

Reference on request

Synopsis of Resume:

MELVIN J. HAMILTON

879 WILSHIRE ROAD
LOWELL, MA 01835
(617) 986-4966

JOB OBJECTIVE: Programming or supervisory position

EXPERIENCE:

1988–Present
Coordinating and Scheduling Analyst
Martin Co., Lowell, MA
Manufacturer of helicopters

1984–88
Systems Analyst
Curtiss Electronics Corporation, Boston, MA
Manufacturer of electronic equipment

1982–84
Group Leader (Computer Operations)
General Copy Corporation, Boston, MA
Left to accept position above.

1979–82
Senior Computer Operator
Newark Power Company, Newark, NJ
Left to accept position above.

EDUCATION:

1974–78
University of Rochester, Rochester, NY
B.S. in Computer Science

1973
Computer Learning Center, Madison, NJ
Certificate of graduation. Courses in programming
and operations. Proficient in COBOL, Assembly, and
FORTRAN languages.

INTERESTS: Sailing; bridge; boat building

AFFILIATIONS: Lowell Yacht Club; Chamber of Commerce;
University of Rochester Alumni Association

MILITARY SERVICE: Army National Guard member since 1974
Present rank: Sergeant First Class

(FOR AMPLIFICATION, SEE FOLLOWING.)

Amplified Resume:

Melvin J. Hamilton
-Page 2-

EMPLOYMENT HIGHLIGHTS

1988–Present
Martin Co.
Coordinating and Scheduling Analyst responsible for projecting future machine schedules, coordinating new systems in operations sections, and explaining new systems and procedures in operations sections.

Help install a new numbering system for reports and machine runs; assign reports and run numbers to new, recurring, or one-time jobs. Utilize full knowledge of each system's operation and purpose. Provide statistical information to operations supervisor. Develop figures for management budget, rental, machine usage, etc.

$4,000 merit increase each year of employment.

Reason for desiring change: to be discussed at interview.

1984–88
Curtiss Electronics Corporation
Systems Analyst. Develop system for customer requirements; price system for profitable, successful bid; write customer contracts; attend bidders' conferences. Follow operations closely to insure fulfillment of contractual requirements. Make monthly financial evaluations of each contract; evaluate existing systems.

Reason for leaving: Martin Co. made offer that appeared to have great potential.

References available

Synopsis of Resume:

Arnold Bachman

110 Summer Street • Los Angeles, CA 90057 • (213) 542-2114

Objective:

Computer Department Supervisor

Experience:

1989–Present

Hill Manufacturing Company
874 Castille Street, Los Angeles, CA
Department Supervisor

1980–88

Eastern Oil Company
502 Madison Avenue, New York, NY
Computer Operator in Saudi Arabia

1973–80

World Chemical Corporation, Newark, NJ
Computer Operator
(Promoted from stock clerk)

Prior:

Littlestone Steel Company, Hamilton, Ontario, Canada
Miscellaneous duties (part-time/summer employment)

Education:

1986

Computer Learning Center, New York, NY
Courses in Programming (COBOL, ALC., FORTRAN);
Operations (Operating Systems); RPG II; Management

Interests:

Football (participation and spectator); reading

Affiliations:

American Machine Accounting Association

(FOR AMPLIFICATION, SEE FOLLOWING.)

*Company name given precedence over position title, as companies
are well known. This indicates applicant has larger operation responsibility.
Self-education emphasized in lieu of formal education.*

Amplified Resume:

Arnold Bachman
-Page 2-

Employment Highlights

1989–Present
Hill Manufacturing Company
(Industrial textile, interior trim)
Department Supervisor, promoted after six weeks as Computer Operator. Replace obsolete machines, eliminating two verifiers. Reduce work force from fifteen to ten. Retrain staff. Replace unsuitable personnel with more effective operators.

Ensure processing of 43 applications, including accounts receivable and payable, payroll, labor analysis, cost of sales, inventory control, customer mailings, reports, and all time-recording operations.

Maintain departmental efficiency as company expands over 28%. Perform computer operations for two new plants and over 450 employees. Have received a total of $20,000 in merit increases since hire date.

1980–88
Eastern Oil Company
Computer Operator on contract in Saudi Arabia. Supervised material order and supply system for this district; conducted weekly inventory of all items required. Resigned to return to the United States.

1973–80
World Chemical Corporation
Computer Operator (advanced from stock clerk). Operated DOS-based inventory system. Resigned to accept lucrative overseas position.

References available.

Synopsis of Resume:

Christopher O'Reilly, C.P.A.

418 Delancy Place
Omaha, NE 61855
(402) 739 - 2331

Objective: Treasurer or Controller for medium-sized company

Experience:

1990–Present   **Treasurer and Director** (of both company and subsidiary)
Henry Morris Co., Omaha, NE
Lincoln Machinery Co., Lincoln, NE

1983–90   **Vice President, Controller, Secretary**
Bloomington Perforating Co., St. Paul, MN

1980–83   **Senior Accountant** in Public Accounting firm
In charge of audits and tax work
Richard Moriarty & Co., C.P.A., Chicago, IL

1977–80   **Public Accounting**
James Platt, C.P.A., Chicago, IL

Education:

1978–80   **University of Chicago**
Bachelor of Science
Major: Accounting; 3.7 average

1976–78   **Florida Technical Institute,** Jacksonville, FL
Associate Degree
Major: Accounting; 3.5 average

Affiliations: Midwest Chapter C.P.A.; National Institute, C.P.A.

Military Service: Lieutenant (junior grade), U.S. Navy
Honorably discharged 1975

(FOR AMPLIFICATION, SEE FOLLOWING.)

*Normally company dollar volume can be used as an indicator of level
of accounting responsibilities. In this instance company volume
was so small it was omitted in favor of number of employees.*

Amplified Resume:

Christopher O'Reilly
-Page 2-

Employment Highlights

1990–Present
Henry Morris Co. (200 employees)
Multi-plant manufacturer of corrugated or fiber box machinery

> As Treasurer and Director of the company and subsidiary (Lincoln Machinery Co.), control all accounting, company financing, and employees in these fields. Improve informative and permanent records while reducing clerical and administrative salaries by $100,000 per annum.

> **Result:** Substantial increase in company's financial strength.

> **Reason for change:** Desire income commensurate with skill and experience.

1983–90
Bloomington Perforating Co.
Perforated metal (75 employees)

> Vice President, Controller and Secretary responsible for all accounting operations and personnel. Advise on financial aspects of the business.

> **Results:** Successful operation and growth of company.

> **Reason for change:** To accept more responsible position with larger company.

References available on request.

Synopsis of Resume:

Luis Suarez

---

33 Fountain Street • Elgin, IL 60102 • (312) 793 - 5357

Objective:

Position in Accounting utilizing supervisory experience, with potential for long-term benefits

Experience:

1990–Present

Night Auditor
Brookside Club & Restaurant, Elgin, IL

1980–89

Business Manager—Corporate Director
Garden Photo Engraving, Inc., Mineola, NY
Company liquidated.

Education:

Hofstra University, Hempstead, NY
Major: Business/Bookkeeping/Accounting
G.P.A.: 3.6

Skills:

Various computer systems

Interests:

Ice skating; fishing; spectator sports

Affiliations:

Administrative Management Society

Free to relocate.

(FOR AMPLIFICATION, SEE FOLLOWING.)

"Displaced" by relocation following termination of lengthy employment.
Overqualified for present position, which is consequently given short shrift.

Amplified Resume

Luis Suarez
-Page 2-

Employment Highlights

January 1990–Present
Brookside Club & Restaurant

Interim position as night auditor for large, prestigious club. Responsible
for auditing all customer tickets for food and beverage daily. Read out the cash
registers and balance sales for the day to register readout. Write up daily report
of all business transacted for the day.

Reason for desiring change: Seek position appropriate to extensive
experience in accounting and supervision.

1980–89
Garden Photo Engraving Co., Inc.

General Business Manager, promoted from Administrative Assistant. Was responsible for all finances of the corporation: banking, accounts receivable and payable,
and taxes. Handled government classified material requiring "secret" security
clearance. Supervised credit manager, bookkeeper, and clerks. Kept detailed records
of sales and balanced all books monthly. Instituted and managed computer system
used by accounting department.

Reason for leaving: Company liquidation.

References available. Please do not contact present employer until after interview.

Synopsis of Resume:

Michael T. Rossi

84 Welling Avenue
Richmond, VA 23225
(703) 262 - 4876

Job Objective: Credit Supervisor

Experience:

June 1990–
Present   **ABC Textiles, Inc.** (2,000+ employees)
                  Richmond, VA
                       Assistant Credit Manager

August 1986–
June 1990   **Consolidated Foods, Inc.** (1,000 employees)
                  Elizabeth City, VA
                       Credit Manager

Prior: Part time during college and summers:
                       Milo Manse, CPA, Palo Alto, CA

Education:

September 1982–
June 1986   **Stanford University,** Palo Alto, CA
                       Degree: B.S. in Business Administration
                       Major: Accounting
                       Honors: Graduated Cum Laude
                       Activities: Debating; Honorary Business Fraternity

Other: **University of Richmond,** Richmond, VA
                       Course sponsored by National Credit Foundation

Interests: Skeet; horseback riding

Affiliations: National Association of Credit Men;

Civic Organizations: Volunteer accounting services to various civic organizations

---

Will relocate for the proper opportunity.

(FOR AMPLIFICATION, SEE FOLLOWING.)

Both major employments for nationally known companies; therefore, company name given precedence over position title. Applicant shows results of effort as indicated by salary more than doubling.

Amplified Resume:

Michael T. Rossi
-Page 2-

Employment Highlights

June 1990–Present
ABC Textiles, Inc.
Hold full authority in extending credit to seven figures and handling substantial portion of company's prospective and actual accounts. Manage accounts of textile wholesalers located throughout the United States, Canada, Mexico, and South America. Utilize thorough knowledge of foreign and domestic credit problems. Grant credit on basis of financial statements and past credit record. Advise customer firm or business on policies andprocedures. Network with hundreds of companies throughout North and South America.

Supervise ten members of credit department; employ full authority when accounts become delinquent. Work closely with sales force; suggest likely prospects and notify sales force of trouble areas.

Salary has more than doubled during employment with ABC.

Reason for desiring change: Wish to advance to supervisory position; no vacancy expected in present firm for several years.

August 1986–June 1990
Consolidated Foods, Inc.
Credit Manager (promoted from Assistant Credit Manager; promoted from Credit Clerk)

Work and responsibilities similar to above on smaller scale. Managed domestic accounts, including jobbers, distributors, and wholesale groceries.

Reason for leaving: To broaden experience with larger company.

References available on request.

Synopsis of Resume:

Lynn Zimmerman

304 Sutton Place
Des Moines, IA 50311
(515) 982 -7650

Objective: Position in consumer lending

Experience:

Jan. 1990–Oct. 1992   **Savings Counselor**
Midland Savings and Loan, Kansas City, MO

Aug. 1987–Sept. 1990   **Supervising Teller**
United Jersey Midstate Bank, Aberdeen, NJ

Education:

1983–1987   **Rosemont College**, Rosemont, PA
B.A. in Business Administration

Other: Night courses: computer operations, word processing,
effective communication

Interests: Aerobics; golf

(FOR AMPLIFICATION, SEE FOLLOWING.)

*Applicant has resigned from two jobs because spouse was
transferred by his company. Applicant emphasizes ability,
experience, and desire for own career.*

Amplified Resume:

Lynn Zimmerman
-Page 2-

Employment Highlights

Jan. 1990-Oct. 1992
Midland Savings and Loan

Savings Counselor in large savings and loan institution with 400 employees and assets over $1.8 billion.

Explained to potential clients the types of savings plans available. Counseled as to most feasible plan. Opened new accounts, preparing all attendant forms and explaining banking procedures to ensure good customer relations in future. Quickly resolved customer problems with courtesy and tact.

Opened over 700 new accounts during tenure; receive 40% salary increase.

Reason for leaving: family relocation

Aug. 1987 - Sept. 1990
United Jersey Midstate

Supervising Teller, promoted from management trainee, responsible for department of ten employees handling all teller functions. Additionally acted as customer service representative with full responsibility for consumer loans, opening new accounts, branch audits, and requisition of all supplies.

As trainee, analyzed financial statements, collateral record postings, credit investigations, checking and savings account maintenance, and beginning teller level-one procedures.

Reason for leaving: family relocation

References on request.

Synopsis of Resume:

Dorothy Ferguson

82 Gifford Street
Falmouth, MA 02540
(617) 335 - 8720

Job Objective: Private-duty Nursing Assistant

Experience:

1990–Present   **National Home Health Care,** Falmouth, MA
                        Major provider of health care services.
                                Nursing Assistant—Visiting Nurse Association certification

1981–89   **Falmouth Pennysaver,** Falmouth, MA
                        Weekly newspaper
                                Typesetter; Compugraphic Operator

Prior: Stenographic and secretarial work at Columbia
                        University, American Airlines, and office temp, 1958–68

Education:

1989–90   **Vocational-Technical School,** Boston, MA
                                Nursing Assistant Certificate
                                One-year course covered patient personal care; taking
                                vital signs; emergency techiques; feeding; CPR; psychology;
                                general geriatric and patient care.

                                Included nine weeks hands-on hospital and nursing-
                                home training under supervision of two registered nurses.
                                In addition, learned report writing and noting detailed
                                observation of patient's condition.

1958–68   **Columbia University,** New York, NY
                                B.A. in Liberal Arts

1954–58   **Central High,** Detroit, MI
                                High school diploma; typing/shorthand award

Interests: Reading; church choir and activities; music

Affiliations: Daughters of American Revolution; Girls' Club Auxiliary

(FOR AMPLIFICATION, SEE FOLLOWING.)

*Mature woman who has taken nursing training
and changed careers in her later life.*

Amplified Resume:

Employment Highlights

1990–Present
National Home Health Care
Health care provider to medical facilities, nursing homes, and private homes

Nursing assistant assigned to individual cases. Receive assignment from firm with detailed briefing on patient history and current level of care needed. Cases vary in length from a week to three months and include stroke patients, cardiac patients, burn victims, and severe accident victims.

When assigned to nursing home, operate under supervision of charge nurse. When assigned to private home, operate without on-site supervision; provide detailed report to firm at conclusion of shift.

Assume full responsibility for patient care within specific framework of given instructions. Patient care encompasses bathing, dressing, and personal grooming, assistance with meals, range of joint motion, decubitus ulcer prevention/care, bandaging, monitoring oxygen equipment, etc. Chart patient activity during shift: intake and output of food and liquid, skin tone, changes of mood or attitude, vital signs, and general demeanor.

Keep patient oriented to person, place, situation, and time. Determine patient's interests and/or hobbies for discussions; read to patient; write letters and notes as requested; encourage walks and wheelchair rides where permitted. Have received many letters of appreciation and call-backs from past clients.

Reason for desiring change: Compensation in line with experience and skill

References available.

Synopsis of Resume:

RUTH ROGERS

---

862 Rupert Street • McLean, VA 22101 • (202) 632 - 9844

Objective:	Charge nurse position in medical-surgical unit
Experience:	
1987–Present	**Millville Veterans' Hospital,** Falls Church, VA 1988: Charge Nurse, Paraplegic Unit 1986–88: Staff Nurse, Amputee Unit
1982–86	**Caldwell County Hospital,** Alexandria, VA 1984–86: Surgical Head Nurse 1982–84: Emergency Room Supervisor 1982: Staff Nurse
1978–82	**Mercy Hospital,** Hornell, NY **St. Mary's Hospital,** Rochester, NY Medical-Surgical Staff Nurse
Education:	
1976–78	**University of Michigan,** Ann Arbor, MI Bachelor of Science in Nursing
1974–76	**St. Luke Hospital School of Nursing,** Kalamazoo, MI R.N. Diploma
Other:	Continuing education courses in Geriatrics, Cardiac, Shock
License:	Virginia license # 123456 Expires December 31, 1994
Affiliations:	American Nurses' Association Michigan State Nurse Association University Hospital Nurses' Alumni Association

(FOR AMPLIFICATION, SEE FOLLOWING.)

*An average record polished to appear brighter through emphasis on
ability to cope with change and scrupulously follow orders.*

Amplified Resume:

Ruth Rogers
-Page 2-

Employment Highlights

1987–Present
Millville Veterans' Hospital, Falls Church, VA

Charge Nurse in Paraplegic Unit, promoted after two years' staff duty in Amputee Unit. Supervise all professional personnel assigned to unit, including therapists.

Reason for desiring change: Wish to return to private sector.

1982–86
Caldwell County Hospital, Alexandria, VA

Surgical Head Nurse, promoted from Emergency Room Supervisor, promoted from staff nurse.

Reason for Leaving: To perform private duty nursing for terminally ill family member.

1978–82
Mercy Hospital, Hornell, NY; **St. Mary's Hospital,** Rochester, NY

Medical-surgical staff nurse. Relieved Charge Nurse as needed. Supervised professional and nonprofessional workers dealing with assigned patients. Took histories, made preliminary observations of patients' conditions, and prepared them for medical treatment and surgical procedures. Observed symptoms and noted results of medical and nursing treatment. Attended to personal needs of patients; administered special diets, medicines, treatments, and dressings. Prepared equipment for treatment and tests. Instructed patients in home care. Kept records and noted irregularities relating to dispensing of narcotics.

Reason for leaving: Family relocation

References on request.

Synopsis of Resume:

WARNER WALKER

---

553 Couch Street   •   Portland, OR 97209   •   (503) 229-9050

JOB OBJECTIVE: Utilize paramedic training and experience in office environment with several private physicians

EXPERIENCE:

1991-Present	SOUTH COUNTY FIRE DEPARTMENT, Portland, OR Journeyman Firefighter/Paramedic
1985–91	LANTERN ELECTRIC CO., Portland, OR Estimator-bidder—promoted from electrician's helper
1984–85	RAYBRO ELECTRIC CO., Baker, OR Front office—promoted from stock clerk

EDUCATION:

1980–84	BAKER HIGH SCHOOL, Baker, OR
Other:	**Part-time vocational school.** Evening courses **Emergency Medical Tech. Course I—200 hours** **Emergency Medical Tech. Course II—500 hours**

LICENSES: Pilot licenses for fixed wing and rotary craft

INTERESTS: Flying; scuba diving; skiing; chess

AFFILIATIONS: State Firefighters' Association

(FOR AMPLIFICATION, SEE FOLLOWING.)

Applicant emphasizes experience and
independence in emergency situations.

Amplified Resume:

Warner Walker
-Page 2-

PARAMEDIC EXPERIENCE

1991–Present
SOUTH COUNTY FIRE DEPARTMENT
(Combined Fire and Ambulance Rescue Service)
Journeyman Firefighter

Because of unique operation combining fire and ambulance services, county offers firefighters free medical technician training at local vocational school and hospitals.

Graduate of Emergency Medical Technician's Course I, stressing emergency care, maintenance of airway, control of bleeding, shock management, emergency baby delivery, and basic life support.

Graduate of Emergency Medical Technician's Course II, stressing scene evaluation, cardiopulmonary resuscitation, intubation, defibrillation, IVs, medication, and advanced life support.

Teach firefighter apprentices basic first aid, standard firefighting duties, and ambulance response. In the field, provide emergency medical care according to physician's radioed instructions; function with minimal supervision and backup.

Reason for desiring change: Wish to make full-time use of medical skills.

References on request.

Cheryl Larson

9009 Fox Street
Denver, CO 80204
(303) 874-7588

Job Objective: Position in the Cardiopulmonary Department. Flexible, willing to learn through new experiences and advanced studies in present or related fields.

Education:
1989–91

Hillsview Junior College, Colorado Springs, CO
Associate degree in Respiratory Therapy

Courses included Airway Management; Artificial Ventilation Therapy; Cardiopulmonary Resuscitation; Chest Physiotherapy; Emergency Procedures; and General Patient Care.

1991–Present

St. Joseph Hospital, Denver, CO
Classroom and laboratory training augmented with hospital orientation. Started as Respiratory Therapy Technician Trainee in work-study program.

Experience:
1991–Present

St. Joseph Hospital, Denver, CO
Employed part-time as Respiratory Therapy Technician III.

Perform therapy and EKG duties: ventilator installation, blood tests, pulmonary function studies, breathing treatments.

Active on "Code Blue" team. Give outpatient instruction on proper breathing techniques; attend emergency pacemaker placement; and assist in stress testing and holter-monitor fitting.

Interests: Skiing; biking; hiking; camping

Affiliations: Denver Ski Club; Young Republicans

References on request.

Student record with limited employment and good training. Has more punch by deleting synopsis.

Synopsis of Resume:

Dorothy L. Hopkins

603 Murray Street
Little Rock, AR 72219
(501) 371-1832

Job Objective: Dental Hygienist in Periodontal Field

Education:

1984   **University of Tennessee**, Memphis, TN
College of Dentistry—School of Dental Hygiene
Graduated with honors in top third of class

Other: **Hendrix College**, Conway, AR

Continuing workshops in special areas to fulfill requirements
of dental hygienist license renewal. Courses included basic
sciences, dental and clinical sciences, and dental technology.
Classroom and clinical instruction required.

Experience:

1985–Present   **George A. Johnson, D.D.S. —Periodontist**
900 W, Markan Street, Little Rock, AR
Dental hygienist in office with four full-time and three
part-time employees. Excellent relationship with doctor as
well as patients.

1984–85   **Wallace Fowler, D.D.S. —General Practice**
Dental hygienist.
Only hygienist in the office; reported directly to Dr. Fowler.

Affiliations: American Dental Hygiene Society

(FOR AMPLIFICATION, SEE FOLLOWING.)

Better-than -average education in her field; thus it appears ahead of employment.
Amplification stresses experience and dependability.

Amplified Resume:

Dorothy L. Hopkins
-Page 2-

Employment Highlights

1985–Present
George A. Johnson, D.D.S.—Periodontist

A highly skilled, experienced hygienist in office of one of the area's leading periodontists, with myriad duties of specialized nature to be performed without supervision.

Perform oral prophylaxis, as well as some root planing and curettage. Place and remove periodontal dressings; give postoperative instructions. Take blood pressure readings and develop X-rays.

Chart mouths; do cavity and oral cancer surveys. Do fluoride and cleaning treatments; take patient's histories.

Percentage of time is devoted to patient education. This involves staining teeth to reveal plaque; pointing out presence of plaque; emphasizing and demonstrating proper brushing and flossing techniques; and importance of regular home care.

Reason for change: Dr. Johnson is retiring. He may be contacted for reference.

1984–85
Wallace Fowler, D.D.S.—General Practice

Accepted position as dental hygienist performing standard functions: prophylaxis; charting patients' mouths; cavity surveys; taking and developing X-rays; and confirming and making appointments.

Reason for leaving: To accept position in preferred periodontal field.

References on request.

Rosemary London

988 Chapel Street
New Haven, CT 06510
(203) 927-5771

Job Objective: Position as Medical Assistant, 30–35 hours per week, preferably with regular schedule.

Education:
1991

Whittier Vocational School, New Haven, CT
Medical Assistant Program encompassing:

Administrative: Scheduling and receiving patients; obtaining patients' data; maintaining medical records; typing and medical transcription; handling phones and correspondence; office care, management, insurance matters, accounts, collection.
Clinical: Preparing patients for examination; obtaining vital signs; taking medical histories; assisting with treatments; performing routine office lab procedures and electrocardiograms; sterilizing instruments and equipment; instruct patients in preparation for X-ray and tests.

Other: **Community College**, Glenside, PA
Various business and science courses

Special Skills: Typing, medical transcribing, routine bookkeeping, billing notices, collections, interviewing, CPR, EKG, aseptic technique, venipuncture, finger stick, injections, basic laboratory.

**Special
Knowledge:** Diabetes mellitus and insulin. Lectured in field for Medical Assistant program. Invited back as guest lecturer for future classes. Circumstances permitting, desire to become active in instruction of diabetics as part of, or in addition to, Medical Assistant duties.

Certification: National Certification Examination
American Association of Medical Assistants.

(Continued)

Experience:

1974–76   **Connecticut General Life Insurance Company**
Assistant to personnel manager. Screened and interviewed job applicants; took dictation as well as handling correspondence on own; supervised payroll. Reason for leaving: family obligations.

1969–71   **Connecticut General Life Insurance Company**
Employed initially as group insurance contract analyst. Promoted to Production Supervisor, Group Insurance Underwriting, which encompassed training and lecturing as well as setting up and conducting workshops. Reason for leaving: family obligations.

**Community
Involvement:**

1976–91   As member of League of Women Voters, used writing, research, and editorial skills for brochures and press releases. Also lectured and assisted in formation of speaker's bureau.

As Chairwoman of Community Concert Association, responsible for all local arrangements for visiting artists (transportation and accommodations), staging, and union liaison.

Researched dietetic nutrition; organized support group for exchange of information.

General: Seek to enter a new field, fully utilizing former solid experience and newly acquired education and skills. Member of American Association of Medical Assistants.

Will travel and relocate.

References on request.

Synopsis of Resume:

Theresa Rinaldi

12 Shoreham Park • Denver, Colorado 80290 • (303) 297-4292

Job Objective: Overall Restaurant Management (Food and Beverage)

Experience:

1987–Present   **Assistant Chef** (20 kitchen personnel)
White Horse Motor Inn and Restaurant
Mountain View Road, Denver, CO

1983–87   **Manager of Food Preparation for College Students**
Westover College, Sundale, MI
Employed by Corbett Company
60 Fisher Building, Detroit, MI

1981–83   **Chief Steward**
Detroit German Club,
Stillson Street, Detroit, MI

1980–81   **Chef** (Heavy food preparation, no short orders)
Golden Diner
1700 Main Street, Detroit, MI

1979–80   **Supervising Chef** (party and volume luncheon business)
Hilltop Restaurant
Broad Street, Detroit, MI

Training:

1974–79   **Presbyterian College of North Carolina**
Business Administration

Hofbrau Hotel, Stuttgart, Germany
Three-year apprenticeship

Interests: Music; travel; painting

Free to relocate.

(FOR AMPLIFICATION, SEE FOLLOWING.)

Only principal jobs are listed to spotlight skills and wide range of experience. Interim jobs were of lesser importance and to list them would serve no real purpose. Overall record will be discussed in full at interview.

Amplified Resume:

Theresa Rinaldi
-Page 2-

EMPLOYMENT HIGHLIGHTS

1987–Present
White Horse Motor Inn and Restaurant
(Serves 1,500 meals per day with varied menus; single breakfasts to large banquets.)

Employed as Assistant Chef. Supervise overall operation of the kitchen in normal operation. Lay out daily work schedule for 20 personnel; personally prepare all sauces and specialized European dishes for this quality restaurant (considered to be one of the top restaurants in Denver and surrounding area).

Turnover rate of kitchen staff is lower than average for restaurants of similar class. Present employer may be contacted for reference.

Reason for desiring change: Desire position as chef.

1983–87
Corbett Company
Employed by Corbett Co. (contractors for cafeteria and restaurant operation) to manage the student dining operation at Westover College, located in the suburbs of Lansing, Michigan. Planned and scheduled menus; purchased all supplies; hired and trained necessary personnel (usually students —consequently required manipulation of work schedules to fit class times). In addition, kept all records and did own bookkeeping.

Paid per student rate by college, but operated on a cost-plus basis rebating differences (if any) to the school. Restaurant operated efficiently enough to allow hosting of alumni dinners for the first time. Generation of extra profit resulted in refunds to the college every month of operation; reached $4,000 maximum for single month.

Transferred to Auto Dealers Institute, Detroit. Industrial-type cafeteria operation, requiring minimal use of training and skill.

Reason for leaving: Resigned for more challenging position.

1981–83
Detroit German Club
Employed as Chief Steward in charge of all restaurant activity including purchasing. Developed steady banquet and special dinner business which returned substantial profit to club and paid for extensive club improvements. Left for above position.

References on request.

Synopsis of Resume:

Mark J. Sanderson

453 Woodland Road
Grand Rapids, MI, 49509
(616) 530-7350

JOB OBJECTIVE: Position of responsibility with growth potential in hospitality industry

EXPERIENCE:
1986–Present

Merrmac Hotels, Grand Rapids, MI
540 rooms, eight restaurants, lounges and bars
Manager of Guest Services

EDUCATION:
1984–86

Grand Valley State College, Allendale, MI
Degree: B.S. in Hospitality and Tourism
Minor: Social Science
G.P.A.:   **3.9**

Activities: Dean's Advisory Council; Residence Hall Advisor
Honors: Phi Kappa Phi; International Study Scholarship;
               Honor Scholarship; Presidential Scholarship Finalist

1982–1984

North Central Michigan College, Petoskey, MI
Liberal Arts; transferred to above

Other:

Miscellaneous part-time employment to help defray costs:
teaching assistant and tutor; audit clerk; lodge desk clerk

INTERESTS: Furniture refinishing; antiques; cooking

Free to relocate.

(FOR AMPLIFICATION, SEE FOLLOWING.)

Resume technique shows progression in one-job employment history.

Amplified Resume:

Mark J. Sanderson
-Page 2-

EMPLOYMENT HIGHLIGHTS

1986–Present
Merrmac Hotels

1992
Promoted to Guest Services Manager with responsibility for 48 employees. Supervise bell stand, valet parking, front desk, and special guest services. Oversee VIP guest arrangements: meeting, greeting, press releases, special menus, beverages, floral arrangements, and other special services.

Establish employee task force to discuss and resolve problems. Initiate special training programs as needed. Solicit employee feedback on policies. Review employee performance on regular basis and issue evaluation reports to management.

1988
Promoted to Night Clerk/Auditor. Principal responsibilities: maintenance of computer system; auditing of cashier and bank reports; resolving guests' complaints; supervision of staff of five; and generating statistics and information regarding daily sales for distribution to General Manager and miscellaneous executives.

1986
Hired initially as desk clerk with following responsibilities: registering all hotel guests; posting charges to guest accounts; making room assignments; and assisting in making future room reservations. Bonded as cashier; position required knowledge of computer system and maintenance of computer records.

Reason for desiring change: Career move to larger market.

References on request. Please do not contact present employer until after interview.

Synopsis of Resume:

Jennifer Marks

843 Oakland Beach
Rye, New York 10580
(914) 849-9906

OBJECTIVE:	Executive or Legal Secretary

EXPERIENCE:

1989–Present	**Amalgamated Productions, Inc.,** New York, NY Motion Pictures and Television Production Administrative Assistant to the President
1986–89	**NDA Broadcasting,** New York, NY Executive Secretary to Vice President
1983–86	**American Brands, Inc.,** New York, NY Administrative Assistant—Legal Department
1980–83	**Potomac School,** McLean, VA Business Practice Teacher
Other:	Miscellaneous vacation jobs to help defray college expenses: legal stenographer, courthouse clerk, resort desk clerk, tour guide

EDUCATION:

1980	**Western Michigan University,** Kalamazoo, MI B.S. in Political Science—Minor: Business Dean's list all four years
Other:	Special courses in speed reading and writing; paralegal seminars
SKILLS:	Typing, shorthand, word processing, speech writing, editing
INTERESTS:	Reading; French cooking

Free to travel and relocate.

(FOR AMPLIFICATION, SEE FOLLOWING.)

Amplified Resume:

Jennifer Marks
-Page 2-

EMPLOYMENT HIGHLIGHTS

1989–Present
Amalgamated Productions, Inc.
> Hired as Office Assistant. Set up and organized office; purchased office
> supplies, machines, and filing cabinets; organized computer network. Promoted to
> Assistant to the Story Editor after one year with substantial salary increase.
>
> Did "first reading" of scripts; participated in story conferences, made recommendations as
> to final selections; assisted in editing and proofing finished products. In 1991 made
> Administrative Assistant to the President. Handled all correspondence and travel
> arrangements; screened calls; prepared status and expense reports; approved bills and
> initiated payments according to contracts.
>
> Operated independently during frequent absences of the president. Given authority to
> exercise judgment and make decisions in many critical areas.
>
> **Reason for leaving:** Wish to work in smaller organization.

1986–89
NDA Broadcasting
> In capacity as executive secretary to vice president in charge of business affairs, prepared
> and issued contracts and payment authorizations for talent and staff involved in TV
> productions. Handled all details of producers' expenses; approved bills and prepared
> expense reports. Left to accept above position with growth potential.

1983–86
American Brands, Inc.
> As administrative assistant in Legal Department, had full responsibility for myriad of
> financial transactions and paperwork inherent in this position. Worked closely with bank
> employees, sales representatives, and general public. Left to enter media field.

1980–83
> Upon graduation from college, accepted interim teaching position in metropolitan area in
> order to become oriented in larger markets. Left for position in New York City.

References on request.

Synopsis of Resume of:

Peter Dixon

45 Barnes Avenue • Memphis, TN 38111 • (901) 863-2819

Job Objective: Purchasing Agent or position leading to it in near future

Experience:

1986–Present   **National Dynamics Corporation**
                    1800 Cruger Avenue, Memphis, TN
                    Buyer of Mechanical Components

1983–86   **Lewin Manufacturing Company** (Office furniture & supplies)
                    1328 Taft Avenue, Atlanta, GA
                    General Purchasing Agent

1978–83   **Schultz Fabricators** (Plastic fabricators)
                    East Main Street,   Atlanta, GA
                    Purchasing Agent

1974–78   **White Company, Inc.** (Hospital equipment manufacturers)
                    Corporate Lane, Nashville, TN
                    Metals Buyer

Education:

1974   **Brothers Institute**, Indianapolis, IN
                    M.B.A.

**Continuing
Education:**   **Jefferson Institute**, Indianapolis, IN—Machine Shop course
                    Alva Technical School, Nashville, TN—Chemistry (one-year course)
                    Atlanta Institute of Technology—Industrial Management course
                    Memphis Technical School—Metallurgy (one-year course)

Interests: Sports (spectator and participant); duplicate bridge

Affiliations: American Society for Metals; Industrial Buyers Association

                    (FOR AMPLIFICATION, SEE FOLLOWING.)

Type of material purchased is mentioned, as well as approximate size of company, to show applicant's level of purchasing responsibility. Yearly income (despite increases) is in lower bracket; therefore mention of it is avoided.

Amplified Resume

Peter Dixon
-Page 2-

EMPLOYMENT HIGHLIGHTS

1986–Present
National Dynamics Corporation (2,000 employees)

Employed as buyer of Mechanical Components in the Electronics Division, with direction over two expediters. Operate on own responsibility, locate suppliers, issue orders without supervision. Nearly all work in the division is on government contract with time and quality paramount. Consequently, the object is to obtain materials consistently up to specifications from firms that can be depended upon for delivery.

Travel to vendor's plants throughout the United States checking facilities; keep records that are referred to when placing orders. Read blueprints and interpret production orders to insure delivery of all materials in correct sequence, avoiding production delay.

Purchase such materials as panels, springs, hinges, chassis, and metal cabinets. Familiar with metals and plastics, and accustomed to ordering to extremely close tolerances. Replaced two buyers (metal components and hardware) and have done the work of both.

Results: Consistently received proper material with very low percentage of rejects. Ten buyers were recommended for salary increases at last evaluation period; was one of two selected for increase.

Reason for desiring change: To acquire a a position of greater responsibility.

1983–86
Lewin Manufacturing Company (700 employees)

As General Purchasing Agent was responsible for four buyers and entire purchasing activity. Purchasers were in substantial seven figures, from vendors in southern and midwestern U.S.

Reason for leaving: To accept growth position in larger firm.

1978–83
Schultz Fabricators (300 employees)

General Purchasing Agent, also in charge of inventory control. Approached by above firm and offered more responsible position.

References available.

Synopsis of Resume:

JEANETTE McDONOUGH

305 Smull Avenue
North Caldwell, NJ 07006
(201) 943-9876

OBJECTIVE: Administrative Secretary or Assistant

EXPERIENCE:
1987–Present   **Caldwell County School System,** North Caldwell, NJ
                           Administrative Secretary

1986–87   **Atwater County School System,** Columbus, OH
                     Administrative Secretary

1983–85   **Malcome & Wrigley**—law firm, Columbus, OH
                     Legal Secretary

Prior: **Fashion Rite Blouses Manufacturing,** Peru, IN
                Assistant to General Manager. Began as apprentice out of high
                school. Intensive overall training in ordering supplies; shipments;
                handling piecework payroll for over 200 employees; preparing
                P & L statements; and income taxes.

EDUCATION: **Bunkerhill High School**, Bunkerhill, IN
                             Commercial Diploma
                             Included training in word-processing equipment

SKILLS: Typing; shorthand; operating dictating machine; word processing

INTERESTS: Physical fitness; crafts; folk music

AFFILIATIONS: Woman's Network (corresponding secretary); church organist
                                and choir director; Boy Scout Parent Support Group

Willing to relocate.

(FOR AMPLIFICATION, SEE FOLLOWING.)

Employing chronology to clarify and highlight solid, somewhat fragmented experience.

Amplified Resume:

Jeannette McDonough
-Page 2-

EMPLOYMENT HIGHLIGHTS

County School Systems

1987–Present Employed in dual capacity as administrative secretary to the Superintendent of Caldwell County schools and to the five-member school board.

Superintendent responsibilities include: making appointments; taking dictation for all business and personal correspondence; handling travel arrangements; balancing expense accounts; issuing vouchers; channeling mail for school system; and general supervision of clerical personnel.

School board responsibilities include travel arrangements; expenses; special notices; and correspondence. Prepare agenda for weekly school board meetings; supervise collation of 200 to 300 packets for distribution to 95 members of school system.

Set up time and location for board meetings; attend meeting and make summary of tape-recorded minutes for distribution at next board meeting. Meet with press personally and on phone to clarify results of weekly meetings as to agenda resolution.

Overall duties include office purchases; budget preparation for school board, school attorney, and Superintendent.

Took special computer training in wordprocessing and have recommended an increase in number of stations for clerical personnel.

Reason for leaving: To obtain position commensurate with skills and experience.

1986–87 Administrative secretary to Superintendent of Schools in Columbus, Ohio. Screened phone calls, handled all business, and composed personal correspondence. Made travel arrangements; prepared agenda for school board and cabinet meetings. Resigned to return to New Jersey.

1985–86 Employed in Caldwell County School System as administrative secretary to the Director of Language Arts and Data Processing. Recommended for promotion to the Superintendent's office. Reason for leaving: family obligations in Ohio.

References on request.

Synopsis of Resume:

BRUCE R. SHEAHAN
87 Kenwood Avenue
New Orleans, LA 70150
(901) 556-7342

Job Objective: Position in Customer Service or Sales Field

Experience:
1991–Present   **Manager of Marketing Administration**
                      Apex Equipment Sales, Inc., New Orleans, LA

1987–91   **Customer Service Representative**
                      Altex Fixture, Inc., Baton Rouge, LA

1984–87   **Salesperson**
                      Morris Sales and Service Co., Hot Springs, AR

1980–84   **Salesperson**
                      Brock-Hall Food Co., Hot Springs, AR

Education:
College courses: **Little Rock University,** Little Rock, AR
                      Evening school courses in Business Administration
                      50 credits acquired toward B. S. degree.

Other: Company-sponsored sales training courses
                      Correspondence courses in Accounting

Affiliations: Sales Executive Club of New Orleans; Rotary International

(FOR AMPLIFICATION, SEE FOLLOWING.)

*Qualifications for present job given focus by position of titles on synopsis sheet,
and credibility is indicated through amplified details.*

Amplified Resume:

Bruce R. Sheahan
-Page 2-

EMPLOYMENT HIGHLIGHTS

1991–Present
Apex Equipment Sales, Inc.
(Manufacturer of dental, surgical, and laboratory equipment)

Employed originally to assist the manager of dental equipment sales section, as well as replace him during yearly month-long vacations and regular trip absences.

Handle all customer correspondence and all inside customer contact by phone or plant visitation. Enter and route all dental equipment orders through plant. Maintain regular contact with twenty-five representatives throughout the southwest.

Retained position through transition period following sale of company to present owners. Promoted to newly created position of Marketing Administration supervising eight personnel in processing all orders entering plant for all products. Yearly dollar volume: low eight figures.

Handle all customer correspondence; revise order handling procedure, resulting in substantial reduction in order handling costs.

Reason for Leaving: Desire position in established organization with low turnover.

1987–91
Altex Fixture, Inc.
(Wood and plastic display equipment)

Employed as Sales Trainee and Apprentice to Sales Engineer. Moved directly into customer sales department with full charge of all order details on repair of returned or defective goods and parts replacement. Remained in same capacity throughout employment, and was retained despite drastic cut in company sales force. Left for above position.

1984–87
Morris Sales and Service Co.
(Distributors of offset and letterpress machines and equipment)

Employed as salesperson covering six-county area. Repeat orders in long-life duplicating machine category infrequent; resigned to handle different product.

References on request.

WILLIAM FREY
752 Sherwood Avenue
Sharon, CT 06069
(203) 643-7792

JOB OBJECTIVE: Position in Sales and/or Demonstrating

EXPERIENCE:

10/90 - 8/91
Demonstrator
Ward Baking Company
29 Clinton Avenue, Sharon, CT

Employed as one of four in area to demonstrate and promote sale of special bakery items (for example, bake-and-serve type rolls), as well as standard production items (bread, pastries, etc.).

With special equipment (oven, etc.), traveled to stores located in small towns in the Sharon, CT, area; stores were of varying size and type with widely varying clientele.

At demonstration worked alone, personally baking most items and offering samples to customers. After samples were consumed, solicited opinions on items, and suggested purchase of them. Sold stock of merchandise which accompanied demonstration; made an impression that would reflect favorably on company and store.

Results:

1. Maintained good volume of merchandise sale.

2. Gained skill in courteously evaluating and handling prospects.

Reason for leaving: Replaced during convalescence from auto accident.

(Continued)

William Frey
- Page 2 -

10/87–9/90
Waiter
Old Spain Restaurant
Sharon, CT

Quality restaurant catering to luncheon trade. Gained experience in meeting and dealing with public, handling money, and coping with various problems posed by diners. Left for position with Ward Baking Company.

1/84–10/87
Salesclerk
Hendricks (stationery store)
Bridgeport, CT

Employed as temporary clerk during special promotion; was offered and accepted permanent position.

Began in card and stationery department. Promoted to office equipment department, selling desks and file cabinets. Had regular contact with business and executive personnel; required good knowledge of items offered as well as proper techniques to consummate sale.

1983–84
Part-time sales clerk

Various part-time salesclerk positions during high school. Sold houseware items, clothing, and garden supplies.

EDUCATION:

Bridgeport High School, CT, 1984

Special Training
Demonstration Training Course given by Ward Baking Company. Gained general training in all phases of store operation during multiple store employment.

Note: Would enter training program if requisite to employment.

All former employers may be contacted for reference.

Minor level of responsibility given added stature through major detail.
Lack of formal education deemphasized through generalization of educational detail.

Synopsis of Resume:

Martin L. Kozlowski
69 Canterbury Road
Corning, NY 14820
(716) 897-4676

OBJECTIVE: Position in field of Marketing or Sales Supervision

EXPERIENCE:
1989–May 1992   **Eastern Sales Manager**
Boyden Equipment Co., 80 Broad Street, Chicago, IL

1982–89   **Assistant to General Sales Manager**
Scovel-Hill, Inc., Schenectady, NY
Moved up from trainee through Sales Staff Group

1979–82   **Assistant to President, Consultant**
Morgan Machine Tool Company, Universal Sports Car Sales,
Foley Farm Equipment Co., Rochester, NY

Prior: Self-employed, owner-manager of appliance company,
Buffalo, NY

EDUCATION:
1968–72   **Niagara University**, Niagara, NY
B.S. in Mechanical Engineering

Other: **University of Buffalo**, evening school
Science courses

U.S. Navy, courses in Industrial Management,
Strategy, Tactics, and Logistics

SERVICE: U.S. Navy Commander in Individual Ready Reserve

AFFILIATIONS: Toastmasters' Club; Rotary; active in local politics

Willing to relocate for the proper opportunity.

(FOR AMPLIFICATION, SEE FOLLOWING.)

*Classical responsibility–result record, reflecting able person quickly taking situation in
hand, assuming additional responsibilities, with corresponding accomplishment.*

Amplified Resume:

Martin L. Kozlowski
-Page 2-

EMPLOYMENT HIGHLIGHTS

1989-1992
Boyden Equipment Company
(Manufacturers of bulk milk cooling equipment)

Employed to direct company's sales effort in New York state, Vermont, Connecticut, New Hampshire, Maine, Ontario, Quebec, and the Maritime Provinces.

Sales are channeled through direct salespeople, manufacturers' representatives, distributors, dealers, and direct major accounts. These include Agway, United Cooperatives of Quebec, and other cooperatives and marketing groups who buy for members. Competition is intense with over 50 competitive firms in the area.

Hired, trained, and directed salespeople; made territorial changes. Selected distributors and dealers, recommended credit limit for final decision by Credit Department. Worked with dealer and distributor personnel, as well as direct salespeople, to aid and stimulate sales effort.

Results:
1. Tripled an original dollar sales volume of low six figures.
2. Increased major direct cooperative accounts from four to ten.
3. Added nine key area distributors, plus seven key dealers.
4. Achieved effective distribution in all Canadian areas.
5. Company valuation of services indicated by an increase of
    $10,000 on a substantial starting yearly income.

Reason for change:
Resigned to seek general manager position unavailable in company.

References available.

Synopsis of Resume:

Sandra Rich-Carhart
410 Younger Road
Sarver, PA 16055
(412) 933 - 8740

JOB OBJECTIVE: Key position in sales capacity where achievement and communication skills will lead to enhanced opportunities and advancement.

EXPERIENCE:

1991–Present **Chlorinator Replacement Parts, Inc.,** Pittsburgh, PA
Manufacturer and Sales Representative

1989–91 **American Telephone Company,** Syracuse, NY
Long-distance service Sales Representative

1988–89 **Wordflow Systems, Inc.,** Syracuse, NY
Service Representative for copiers

1983–88 **Syracuse Girls Club,** Syracuse, NY
Recreational Program Aide

Prior: Volunteer work for Red Cross, hospital, PTA; teaching aide

EDUCATION:

1976 Syracuse High School; worked summers as retail sales clerk in local department store.

Other: Seminars and workshops in sales and marketing

AFFILIATIONS: American Marketing Club; Pittsburgh Sales Association

INTERESTS: Karate; jogging

(FOR AMPLIFICATION, SEE FOLLOWING.)

Amplified Resume:

Sandra Rich-Carhart
-Page 2-

EMPLOYMENT HIGHLIGHTS

1991–Present
Chlorinator Replacement Parts, Inc.

Manufacturer, dealer, and distributor of parts used in equipment that purifies drinking and waste water.

Set up new sales division. Design and write promotional material and brochures. Research state for prospective customers.

Deal principally with municipalities, state institutions, and county governments as well as limited number of private companies. Make "cold calls" to determine persons in charge of ordering and purchase (city mayors to plant operators).

Set up sales structure and weekly itinerary; sell parts; give quotations; schedule repair-work.

On the road approximately four days a week covering territory of approximately 3,000-mile radius. Increased sales over 25% with no prior experience with product.

Reason for desiring change: Upward career move to use communication skills more fully.

1989–91
American Telephone Company

Employed as sales representative for this long-distance service company. Generated all leads; handled direct sales and customer relations. Trained new sales personnel; named "Top Salesperson of Year" in 1990. Left for position above.

1988–89
Wordflow Systems, Inc.

Employed as customer service representative making "cold calls" on potential customers to set up demonstration of copier equipment. Worked with customers to determine appropriate equipment needs. Left for position above.

References available on request.

Synopsis of Resume:

FRED G. SNOW

418 West Street
Pittsburgh, PA 15235
(412) 303-6224

JOB OBJECTIVE: Position in retail management field—department store or
comparable operation

EXPERIENCE:

1991–Present   **Merchandising Manager**
R.S. Wilson Department Store
West Broadway, Pittsburgh, PA

1982–91   **Store Manager** (up through the ranks from salesperson)
Ward, Roebuck & Co., New York, NY
Yearly income increased to $40,000 during employment.

EDUCATION:

1980   **Lincoln High School**, Providence, RI

1980–82   **Carnegie Business College**, Pittsburgh, PA
2-year course in Business Management included Accounting,
Auditing, Bookkeeping Economics, and Finance

AFFILIATIONS: American Legion; YWCA

INTERESTS: Painting; music; theater

(FOR AMPLIFICATION, SEE FOLLOWING.)

*Salary mentioned in previous rather than present employment to alert
prospective employer to earning bracket without pinpointing amount.*

Amplified Resume:

Fred G. Snow
-Page 2-

EMPLOYMENT HIGHLIGHTS

1991–Present
R.S. Wilson Department Store

Employed as Merchandise Manager with complete responsibility for all merchandising for entire store (composed of approximately 50 departments).

Reason for leaving: Desire position in progressive retail environment.

1982–91
Ward, Roebuck & Company

Originally employed as salesclerk in Housewares Department of Providence branch. Promoted in six months to Manager of the Men's and Boys' Clothing Department. Promoted in eighteen months to Assistant Manager in charge of 50 employees.

Promoted to Assistant Manager in Charge of Operations at Boston branch. Had charge of all operational functions.

Promoted to Store Manager at Allentown, PA branch with 35 employees.

Promoted to Manager of Scranton, PA branch. In 10 months increased volume by 35% and was rated "Potential District Manager" material on annual evaluation.

Promoted to Regional Merchandiser for 115 stores, supervising Women's Ready-to-Wear, Domestic and Yard Goods, Men's and Boy's Hosiery, and Curtains and Drapes departments.

Promoted to Manager of Baltimore branch with 100 to 125 employees. Managed store from June 1990 to April 1991. Increased store's yearly volume over $550,000. Decreased employee turnover; improved housekeeping department.

Reason for leaving: Accepted position offered by R.S. Wilson Department Store.

References available.

Synopsis of Resume:

Dudley M. Howard
987 Culver Avenue
Burlington, VT 05401

Job Objective: Position in Sales Management on District or Regional level

Experience:
1991–Present   **Haley Car Company,** Burlington, VT
                  Appraiser and salesperson

1985–91   **Mansfield Motors,** Rutland, VT
                  Sales Manager

1978–82   **Rutland Motor Sales,** Rutland, VT
                  Salesperson

1976–78   **Valley Cars, Inc.,** Shrewsburg, VT
                  Service Manager

1974–76   **Lakeport Marine Company,** Lakeport, NH
                  Salesperson

Education:
                  State University of Maine, Orono, ME
                        Have acquired 60 credits toward a B.A. in
                        Business Administration
                        Activities: Advertising manager for college peroidical

1974   **Rockland High School,** Rockland, ME

Other: Sales seminars and workshops

Interests: Photography; amateur radio operator

(FOR AMPLIFICATION, SEE FOLLOWING.)

Points out qualities essential in all sales management: success in personal sales,
coupled with success in getting maximum sales effort when managing salespeople.

Amplified Resume.

Dudley M. Howard
-Page 2-

EMPLOYMENT HIGHLIGHTS

1991–Present
Haley Car Company

Appraiser and salesperson. Interim position; present employer aware and may be contacted for reference.

1985-1991
Mansfield Motors, Rutland, VT

Employed initially as salesperson; promoted to Sales Manager in first year.

Hired and trained five new salespersons. Instituted a bonus system to stimulate sales activity. Established a follow-up program requiring each salesperson to call on each car purchaser one week after sale. Salesperson ensured customer satisfaction and obtained names of friends who had seen or driven car; valuable method of building prospects list.

Directed sales promotions, administration, and advertising. Designed advertisments for local papers; developed special promotions. Conceived "Old Timers' Parties" where former customers (now on inactive list) received special invitations to new car shows.

Results:

As Salesperson—Increased sales by over 30% first year.

As Sales Manager—Showed increases of over 35% each year. Increased sales from 14 cars per month in 1986 to 50 in 1991. Agency rose from ninth to third in sales in the country.

Reason for leaving: Company reorganization.

References available on request.

Synopsis of Resume:

HUGH STELJES

120 Farley Street
Indianapolis, IN 46421
(317) 611-9044

JOB OBJECTIVE: Supervisory position in drafting or work leading to such a position

EXPERIENCE:
1988–Present   DRAFTER
                    Electronic Communications, Incorporated
                    200 Front Street, Indianapolis, Indiana

1980–88   Interim employment during education
                    Ace Vending Machine Company, Jefferson City, Missouri
                    Employed by District Manager to repair machines at home.

                    Miller Parts & Equipment Company, Jefferson City, Missouri
                    Repaired heavy equipment (tractors, industrial equipment, etc.).

EDUCATION:
1987–89   **Bates Technical Institute**, Jefferson City, Missouri
                    Took evening courses in Basic Electronics, Descriptive Geometry,
                    Trigonometry, and Drafting.

1980–84   **Salem High School**, Salem, Missouri
                    Jefferson City High School, Jefferson City, Missouri
                    Took drafting courses, including college-level courses in
                    Architectural Drafting.

INTERESTS: Music; do-it-yourself repair projects

AFFILIATIONS: YMCA

(FOR AMPLIFICATION, SEE FOLLOWING.)

One-job background requiring thorough coverage to expose all capabilities.

Amplified Resume

Hugh Steljes
-Page 2-

EMPLOYMENT HIGHLIGHTS

1988–Present
Electronic Communications, Inc.

Employed originally as Drafter III. Learned company systems; handled small detail drawings, electrical and mechanical.

Promoted to Drafter II. Prepared fabrication or detail drawings required for manufacturing purposes. Worked with designers and engineers under minimum supervision. Also worked from sketches, designs, or layouts.

Frequently given a rough sketch of a part or assembly of parts with only main or overall demensions specified. Required to locate tubes, switches, other electronic or mechanical parts. Made detail drawings of each element using dimensions drawn from company tolerances and engineering specifications, keeping whole package within overall dimensions required.

Selected as lead drafter for specifications control and procurement outline drawings coverage on a multimillion-dollar missile project. Familiarity required with Ordnance and General Electric Corporation systems of drawing and procedures. Authorized to select parts or units that fit overall specifications. Made drawings of parts to be purchased; handled correspondence with vendors. Also handled correspondence with Ordnance and Contract Associates on matters pertaining to specifications. Expert in government procedures and specifications.

Promoted to Drafter I during above assignment; now designing small units while continuing aforementioned responsibilities.

Reason for desiring change: Wish to progress into management.

References available.

Synopsis of Resume:

Louis Da Silva
80 Brett Street
Seattle, WA 98101
(206) 743-7635

OBJECTIVE: Electronics Designer or Drafter

EXPERIENCE:
1990–Present   **Electronics Drafter (Design)**
                    Farrel Photo, Incorporated, Seattle,WA

1982–90   **Project Drafter (electrical and mechanical)**
                    National Electronics, Phoenix, AZ
                    Victor Design, Inc., Farmington, NM
                    Standard Products, Inc., Santa Barbara, CA
                    Morris Electronics, Los Angeles, CA
                    Milo Corporation, Barstow, CA
                    Simco Electric Co., Tucson, AZ
                    Western Conductor Sales, Spokane, WA
                    Burns Electronics, Burns, OR

EDUCATION:
1983–88   Continuing education courses in Basic Engineering, Mechanical
                    Drawing and Engineering, Mathematics and Physics for Mechanical
                    Engineering, and Electronics

1982   **West High School**, Seattle, WA

INTERESTS: Bowling; hunting; fishing

Free to relocate; willing to travel; would accept overseas post.

(FOR AMPLIFICATION, SEE FOLLOWING.)

This resume demonstrates project or short-term employment technique. It gives a logical
reason for extraordinary number of job changes. It combines the multiple employments into a clear, credible list.

Amplified Resume:

Louis Da Silva
Page 2

EMPLOYMENT HIGHLIGHTS

1990–Present
Farrel Photo Incorporated (350 employees)
Manufacturers of photographic and microfilming apparatus

> Responsible for design, layout, and detailing of schematics and wiring diagrams for various devices produced for U.S. Army and U.S. Navy. Reason for leaving: current government contracts expire in 1993; incoming contracts do not utilize expertise.

1990–92 Project Assignments

National Electronics
> Large manufacturer of electronic devices. Worked with company engineers and drafters in layout and classified equipment to be used in the early warning and missile systems.

Victor Design, Incorporated
> Major manufacturer of air conditioning equipment. Responsible for design and layout of electrical wiring for commercial production.

Standard Products, Incorporated
> Manufacturer of heavy-duty machine tools. Assisted in mechanical design and layout of extrusion presses.

Morris Electronics
> Manufacturer of crossbar switches, scanners, and monitors. Assigned to design and layout of electronic devices.

Milo Corporation, Simco Electric Company, Western Conductor Sales
> Manufacturers of portable and mobile testing equipment for missile and aircraft industries; electronic components for missile, aircraft, radio, and television industries.

> In above projects, duties involved layout; design of electromechanical parts and devices for ground support of drone target planes; and modernization of obsolete drawings and pictorial view of components for mechanical and electrical parts lists.

Burns Electronics
> Manufacturer of missiles and component parts. Revised old drawings, detailed new layouts. Sketched schematics, wiring diagrams, pictorial drawings, electrical parts lists, and detailed instruments panels.

References on request.

Synopsis of Resume:

DONALD FREER

27 Meigs Street
Olympia, WA 98501
(507) 366-3228

JOB OBJECTIVE: Technical position in electronics field with growth opportunity

EXPERIENCE:
1990–Present   **Manville-Forbes Company,** Portland, OR
Service engineer for North America
NOTE: Continuation of employment below;
Ace Automation purchased by Manville-Forbes Co.

1988–90   **Ace Automation,** Culver City, CA
Service manager

1982–87   **Borgman Corporation,** Sacramento, CA
Supervisor of mechanical maintenance

Prior: **Keller Ford Agency,** Carson City, NV
Auto mechanic, radio repairperson

U.S. Forestry Service
Mechanic supervising repair of road-building equipment

General: Can operate or repair any type of machine in a standard
machine shop.

EDUCATION:
1987   **Franklin Technical Institute,** Geyser, NV
Machine design major

Other: **Culver Institute of Technology,** Sacramento, CA
Evening courses in Industrial Management

LaSalle Technical Institute, New York, NY
Radio and Electronics correspondence courses

INTERESTS: Hunting; fishing; model railroading

Free to relocate.

(FOR AMPLIFICATION, SEE FOLLOWING.)

Amplified Resume:

Donald Freer
Page 2

EMPLOYMENT HIGHLIGHTS

1988–Present
Manville-Forbes Company / Ace Automation

Employed originally by Ace Automation to service and install electrically operated continuous weighing systems produced by the company.

Retained during buy-out by Manville-Forbes Co. and ultimately promoted to Service Engineer for North America. Supervise each installation; train service people at the local Manville-Forbes offices in all aspects of repair and service.

Results: No record of faulty installations or poor service.

Reason for desiring change: Desire position that does not involve travel.

1982–87
Borgman Corporation

Employed as one of 10 maintenance machinists repairing all types of machine shop equipment.

Promoted to Supervisor of Maintenance of Mechanical Equipment with up to 15 personnel under direction. Responsible for keeping machinery and vehicles operational in plant. Machinery ranged from simple machine shop devices to highly complicated special machines, such as electrical or mechanical equipment used in modern laboratories.

Interviewed and recommended employment of assistants; discharged when necessary. Trained people when skilled personnel were not available. Low turnover.

Reason for leaving: Company reorganization.

References available.

Demonstrates experience in lieu of college.
Steady position climb indicates conscientious application of knowledge acquired on the job.

Synopsis of Resume:

Harold Knowland

876 Highland Drive
Seattle, WA 98013
(206) 972-8762

Job Objective: Design Engineering in Electromechanical Field

Experience:

1989–Present   **General Pacific, Inc.,** Seattle, WA
Machine Designer

1988–89   **Delco Engineering Co.,** Boise, ID
Contract design work

1986–88   **Allstate Tool Machine Co.,** Silver City, ID
Electromechanical design

Prior: **Fotex, Inc.,** Silver City, ID
Drafter

Education:

1988–Present   **University of Washington**
Have acquired 90 credits toward a B.S. in
Mechanical Engineering.

1981–1983   **Silver Springs Institute of Technology,** Silver City, ID
Associate degree in design engineering

Other: Company-sponsored course on automation

Affiliations: Allstate Society of Design Engineers

Interests: Do-it-yourself home projects; music

(FOR AMPLIFICATION, SEE FOLLOWING.)

Amplified Resume:

EMPLOYMENT HIGHLIGHTS

1989–Present
General Pacific, Inc., Seattle, WA
(Mechanical packings and oil seals)
　　Employed as machine designer in a company that requires special machines for unusual products.

　　When given an idea or request for a machine to perform a specified function, make a rough sketch and rough estimate. If approved, make complete layout sketch of the device; a detail worker in the shop prepares the final drawings. Follow through on construction of device in the shop until it is put to actual production use. Have final decision on any suggested change.

　　Results: Have designed 70 machines since joining the company. Several notable successes: impregnated packing, folding and calendering machines; machine to deliver rubber in varying piles; and trimming machines for shaft seal inserts.

　　Reason for desiring change: Wish to relocate to warmer climate.

1988–89
Delco Engineering Co., Boise, ID
　　Employed to perform design work; resigned to accept more challenging position above.

1986–88
Allstate Tool Machine Co., Silver City, ID
　　Employed as detailer. Contacted customers; sketched electromechanical designs, including relay work. Position eliminated during company reorganization.

Prior
　　Radio repair; various jobs as a drafter prior to above employment.

References available.

Synopsis of Resume:

HELMUT L. DAMSKY
22 Tyler Road
Providence, RI 02910
(401) 882-7664

OBJECTIVE: Position in Mechanical Engineering or Design

EXPERIENCE:
1992–Present   **Plant Engineer**
                    National Packaging Corp., Providence, RI

1988–92   **Vice President, promoted from General Manager**
                    Hunter Co. / Neely Equipment Co., Providence, RI

1983–88   **Tool and Die Foreperson**
                    Haverhill Instruments Corp., Trenton, NJ

1980–83   **Tool Room Supervisor**
                    Elgin Machine Corp., New Haven, CT

EDUCATION:
1979–80   **Providence Technical Institute**, Providence, RI
                    Courses in Organic Chemistry and Basic Radio

Other: **Rhode Island College**, Providence, RI
                    Courses in Management, Economics, and Mathematics

                    Continuous self-study program in mechanics, engineering,
                    electronics, and design

LANGUAGES: Working knowledge of Polish and German

INTERESTS: Building stereo components; photography; family activities

AFFILIATIONS: Volunteer firefighter

(FOR AMPLIFICATION, SEE FOLLOWING.)

Details given on most employment only, where important career progress has been made.
Amplifications of lesser employments could detract from impact of more recent responsibilities and accomplishments.

Amplified Resume:

Helmut L. Damsky
Page 2

EMPLOYMENT HIGHLIGHTS

1992–Present
National Packing Corporation
Plant engineer supervising polyethelene extrusion processes plus all mechanical and electrical maintenance.

Hire and train groups totaling 75 personnel for these purposes. Design and redesign equipment for better, more efficient, quality production. Supervise rebuilding; add controls (both electrical and mechanical) for secondhand machinery brought into plant.

Reason for change: Desire managerial position commensurate with experience and skill.

1988–92
Hunter Co. / Neely Equipment Co.
(Manufacturers of equipment used in printing, coating, photo engraving, laminating, and polyethulene extrusion)

Employed originally by Hunter Co. of Providence, RI as mechanical enginer. In 1989, appointed General Manager of Neely Equipment Co., a subsidiary of Hunter Co. In 1990, promoted to Vice President of Neely Equipment Co.

Handled all contact with prospective and established customers; discussed problems, implemented solutions. Made rough sketches of machines or devices, proposed production line sequence. Upon approval made detailed drawings and estimates. After order obtained, supervised production of equipment, set up in customer's plant, followed through to employee training, and ensured customer satisfaction. Photographs and sketches of successful designs created are available for inspection.

Reason for leaving: Company was purchased by above firm; in reorganization, was made plant engineer.

References available on request.

Synopsis of Resume:

Thomas L. Lynn
98 Brooks Avenue
Boston, MA 02646

Job Objective:	Television Engineering Technician
Experience:	
1991–Present	**WFPU-TV (PBS)**, Boston, MA Engineering Technician
1989–91	**Kaymart Productions**, Hollywood, CA Design Engineer assistant
1987–89	**Dell Fill Productions**, Beverly Hills, CA Photographer, Gaffer, Set Builder
Education:	
1983–87	**Boston University**, Boston, MA B.A. in Communications with emphasis on broadcasting, production, and newswriting.
Other:	**Columbia College**, Hollywood, California Courses in film production, sound recording, mixing
Interests:	Skiing; bridge; chess
Affiliations:	Jaycees; Knights of Columbus

(FOR AMPLIFICATION, SEE FOLLOWING.)

Amplified Resume:

Thomas L. Lynn
Page 2

EMPLOYMENT HIGHLIGHTS

1991–Present
WFPU-TV, Boston, MA

Engineering assistant involved with production of documentary films, weekly educational children's program, and live television coverage of centennial. Currently studying for first-class radio/telephone license.

Familiar with:

(1) RCA TK-43 and RCA-44B cameras
(2) RCA TR-70 videotape machine
(3) RCA TCR-100 cartridge videotape machine
(4) RCA TEP editor
(5) Character generator
(6) Camera and film chain; audio and video switching
(7) Studio lighting; operation of remote equipment
(8) Film editing
(9) Copywriting, trailer narration, mixing, gaffing

Reason for leaving: Limited opportunity for advancement

Summary:
All previous experience has contributed to overall knowledge in chosen field. Have personally designed and built custom film editing equipment and projection devices, as well as custom dubbing studio.

References on request. Please do not contact present employer at this time.

Synopsis of Resume:

Ruth Mallory

29 Gillette Street
Richmond, VA 23234
(703) 322-6647

Job Objective: Position as Executive Housekeeper at a hotel, motel, or apartment hotel

Experience:
1990–Present   500-room hotel located in eastern Virginia
Salary plus full maintenance
•Executive Housekeeper

1988–90   **Hotel Wagner**, Norfolk, VA (300 Rooms)
Salary plus full maintenance
•Executive Housekeeper

1986–88   **Chatham Hotel**, Virginia Beach, VA (200 rooms)
Salary (no maintenance)
•Executive Housekeeper

1985   **Sea Chest Hotel**, Ft. Meyers, FL (150 rooms)
Salary plus apartment
•Executive Housekeeper

1983–85   **Normandy Apartment Hotel**, New Orleans, LA (75 rooms)
Salary (no maintenance)
•Executive Housekeeper

Education:
1980   Hillsborough County Vocational-Technical School, Tampa, FL

Special Training: **Murey Hotel Training Course**, Washington, D.C.
Courses in typing and bookkeeping

Interests: Gardening; reading

Affiliations: Executive Housekeepers Association

(FOR AMPLIFICATION, SEE FOLLOWING.)

As position title remains the same, progress is shown through increase in size of establishment.
Because resume is to be widely circulated, actual name of present employer is omitted.
Mail address is that of relative rather than hotel to prevent further identification.

Amplified Resume:

Ruth Mallory
Page 2

Employment Highlights

1990–Present
Executive Housekeeper for one of the leading hotels in eastern Virginia, supervising staff of 62. Interview, hire, train, and discharge. Assign all work; oversee its completion. Keep time cards and records; issue paychecks. Staff turnover minimal.

Complete redecoration and remodeling of the 500-room hotel ongoing throughout employment. Consult and supervise seamstress personnel; meet deadlines on rooms rented but not completely remodeled.

Reason for desiring change: Desire position commensurate with experience and skill.

1988–90 Hotel Wagner (Staff of 40)
Performed executive housekeeping functions similar to above on smaller scale, with added duties peculiar to a convention hotel (such as tearing down bedrooms and remaking them into living rooms). Resigned for position above.

1986–88 Chatham Hotel (Staff of 35)
Temporary position which terminated when former housekeeper returned after leave of absence. Satisfactorily discharged assigned duties despite general employee strike called during tenure.

1985 Sea Chest Hotel (Staff of 20)
Employed as Executive Housekeeper with standard duties, plus full charge of laundry. Position eliminated during company reorganization.

1983-85 Normandy Apartment Hotel (Staff of 20)
Performed executive housekeeping functions on small scale, plus doubling as evening receptionist. Resigned to relocate to Florida.

Prior: Dealt with public in various capacities, including job of head hostess in the main dining room of the Sheraton-Brock Hotel in Niagara Falls, Canada. Successfully operated two restaurants in Florida, one with partner, one as sole owner. Sold both at a profit.

References available.

Synopsis of Resume:

Gary M. Siebert

595 Ocean Boulevard
Sarasota, FL 33581
(813) 922-9875

Job Objective: Driving Instructor

Experience
1989–Present   **Luther's Driving School**, Sarasota, FL
Driving Instructor

1986–89   **Miller Ford**, Bradenton, FL
Used car salesman

1978–86   **Sarasota Public Schools**
Elementary School Teacher

Education
1974–77   **University of Alabama**, Tuscaloosa, AL
B.A. Sociology; minor—Political Science

Skills: Chauffeur's license, private pilot's license

Interests: Tennis; golf; sports car rallying; hang gliding; flying

(FOR AMPLIFICATION, SEE FOLLOWING.)

Changing fields of employment later in career.

Amplified Resume:

Gary M. Siebert
Page 2

EMPLOYMENT HIGHLIGHTS

1989–Present
Luther's Driving School

Instructor of commercial driving school established in this area for 20 years.

Test approximately four students each weekday; occasional weekend work. Student ages range from 17 to 85. Lessons average two hours. Approximately 90% of students pass the driving examination written and road tests on first try.

Reason for desiring change: To be discussed at interview.

Former Employment

Teacher
Taught social studies in public schools. Excellent references and record during tenure.

Car Salesperson
Sold used cars and trucks; named "Top Salesperson" in last year of employment. Amicable separation to accept position that would combine teaching and driving skills.

References available upon request. Present employer may be contacted.

Synopsis of Resume:

Janice R. Eastwood

440 Ridgewood Avenue
Annandale, VA 24422
(703) 987-4557

Job Objective: Retirement Complex Manager

Experience:
1990–Present   **Endicott Retirement Complex,** Annandale, VA
Resident Manager of low-income housing complex (94 units).

Prior: **Busch Gardens,** Williamsburg, VA
Part-time summer employment while in college: guest relations hostess,
hospitality hostess, cashier.

Burrell Home for Adults, Roanoke, VA
Worked with senior citizens in adult home setting. Residents included
ambulatory, non-ambulatory, mentally and physically handicapped.
Developed recreational activities; expanded volunteer program;
counseled residents.

Radford University, Radford, VA
Upon graduation served as social work intern in six-week program.

Education:
1986–90   **Radford University**, Radford, VA
Degree: B.A. in Social Work; Minor in Psychology
Honors: Alpha Delta Mu (National Social Work Honor Society);
Pi Gamma Nu (National Social Sciences Honor Society);
Vice President of National Federal of Student Social Workers

Other: **Institute of Real Estate Management**, 101 Series
Educational requirement for accredited Resident Manager
Designation

Affiliations: League of Older Americans Senior Volunteer Program;
Advisory Council Member; United Way Council Member

Interests: Outdoor sports; needlework; art

Willing to relocate.

(FOR AMPLIFICATION, SEE FOLLOWING.)

Amplified Resume:

Janice R. Eastwood
Page 2

Employment Highlights

1990–Present
Endicott Retirement Complex

Employed by Management Services of Silver Springs, VA as resident manager of 94-unit apartment complex. Responsible for employing and supervising qualified personnel, as well as training and writing performance review of secretary, janitor, and maintenance person.

Ongoing responsibilities include:

(1) Rental of apartments to low-income persons over 62 years of age, and younger disabled persons who meet eligibility criteria of HUD.

(2) Prospective tenant interviews; determination of eligibility; credit and reference checks; rental collections; bank deposits. Purchase janitorial needs and office supplies.

(3) Supervision, general administration and physical operation of complex. After completion of initial occupancy of building, responsible for warranty issues and consultation with general contractor on construction and maintenance issues.

(4) On 24-hour call, charged with successfully meeting and handling all medical and maintenance emergencies. Full charge of all complex social activities and resident relations as well as supervision of staff providing transportation, recreational, and housekeeping services to residents.

(5) Charged with marketing and ultimately leasing all apartments. Advertise and promote elderly housing lifestyle options through bulk mailings and personal presentations to community groups and organizations.

Results: No turnover in immediate staff; tenant morale high; rated "Excellent" on each six-month evaluation with appropriate raise in salary.

Reason for desiring change: Seek larger market with potential for significant advancement.

References available on request. Please do not contact present employer at this time.

Synopsis of Resume:

Peter Avery
530 Marion Avenue
Dallas, TX 78745
(512) 972-0733

Job Objective: Condominium or Apartment Complex Manager in state of Texas

Experience:
1986–Present   **Oak Plaza Villas**, Dallas, TX
Manager of 58 one-story units in three sections of town

1980–86   **Hauser Reality, Inc.,** Fort Worth, TX
Real estate sales and property management

1978–80   **Morgan Department Store**, Gaylord, LA
Clerk to Assistant Buyer

1974–78   Miscellaneous employment as carpenter and construction worker

Education:
1972–74   **Vocational-Technical Institute,** Beaumont, TX
Shop and automotive mechanics

Other: High school; correspondence accounting course; refresher
bookkeeping course nights at community college

Skills: Carpentry; drywall work; plumbing; bricklaying; mechanics

Interests: Making furniture; softball; bowling

Affiliations: Lion's Club; Red Cross Volunteer

Willing to relocate within state of Texas.

(FOR AMPLIFICATION, SEE FOLLOWING.)

Amplified Resume:

Peter Avery
-Page 2-

EMPLOYMENT HIGHLIGHTS

1986–Present
Oak Plaza Villas

Assumed management of administratively disorganized 58-unit complex.

Completely reorganized books; installed new systems of billing, bookkeeping, record keeping, and bill paying. Repaired outdoor furniture in recreation area, erected pool fence, and changed filter system.

Streamlined rental procedures of owner-investor units, requiring application forms complete with current references. Assumed responsibility for checking references as well as interviewing prospects and presenting Board of Directors with findings for final decisions. Handle all banking.

With volunteer resident labor and cooperation, effected complete renovation of recreation room, plus large common area used for meetings and social activities. Repainted, recarpeted, and installed new lighting system both inside and out for improved security; installed bolt locks.

Accept bids for periodic projects such as roofing, septic tank cleaning, and paving for final board decision. Oversee garbage collection and pest control. General troubleshooter in tenant disputes.

Make daily check of laundromat appliances in each of three buildings, as well as evening check for any trouble alert. Field phone calls for proper referrals; organize annual monthly board meetings.

Overall running responsibilities encompass billing, annual report, bookkeeping, collection of delinquent accounts, and assessments.

Reason for desiring change: Desire position with rent-free apartment or condominium in addition to salary.

References on request.

Synopsis of Resume:

JOHN D. FOLEY

756 Tangelo Avenue   •   Orange City, FL 32763   •   (813) 397-7765

Job Objective: Security Guard

Experience:

June 1991–Present   **Lake Woods Retirement Center**, Orange City, FL
          Security guard

1986–91   **Wakefield Corporation**, Orlando, FL
          Polygraph examiner

1959–86   **Department of Police**, Union, NJ
          Patrol officer, promoted to detective, promoted to supervisor

1955–59   **Cummings Photography**, New York, NY
          Commercial photographer

Education: High school graduate; continuous field-related seminars in polygraph
          science, law enforcement, video application for security, and narcotics;
          Firearms Instructors School.

Other: Registered N.R.A. Police Pistol Instructor

Service: U.S. Army, 1952-55

(FOR AMPLIFICATION, SEE FOLLOWING.)

Former police officer using career record as qualification for security job during retirement.

Amplified Resume:

John D. Foley
Page 2

EMPLOYMENT HIGHLIGHTS

June 1991–Present
Lake Woods Retirement Center

Check all persons and vehicles entering complex for proper authorization. Record all information; report any irregularities or disturbances to "round sergeant" who physically checks residence.

Reason for leaving: Seek greater responsibility consistent with background.

1986–91
Wakefield Corporation

State-licensed examiner for detection of deception in polygraphs. Conducted pre-employment, periodic, and specific polygraph examinations for employer's large client roster. Analyzed charts; made critical decisions as to truthfulness or deception.

Reason for leaving: Operation and convalescence.

1959–86
Department of Police, Union, New Jersey

1959: Foot patrol, radio car patrol, motorcycle patrol, and dispatch officer.

1962: Promoted to Detective, Bureau of Criminal Investigation. Established classification system. Police photographer for criminal and accident investigation; court fingerprint expert witness. Two citations for valor in apprehension of two murder suspects.

1982: Promoted to General Supervisor of Record Personnel. Duties encompassed preservation and documentation of physical evidence and property; preparation of forensic material; and investigation and preparation of firearm purchase permits and concealed weapon permits.

Reason for leaving: Retired; relocated to warmer climate.

References and commendations available.

Synopsis of Resume:

Anthony J. Micelli
5007 Bristol Avenue
Sioux Falls, SD 57105
(605) 729-1062

Job Objective:	Superintendent of Construction, or Carpenter's Superintendent
Experience:	
June 1991– Present	**Carpenter** (temporary position) J. Ackerman & Sons, Sioux Falls, SD
June 1989– Dec. 1990	**General Superintendent** ($4 million apartment house) Regal Homes, Inc., Sioux Falls, SD
March 1988– May 1989	**General Construction Superintendent** Hastings Contracting Company, Aberdeen, SD
Jan. 1987– Feb. 1988	**Construction Superintendent** ($1 million apartment house) Lindsay Construction Co., Bismarck, ND
1977– 1986	**General Superintendent, Carpenter Superintendent, Carpenter Foreperson** Blanchard Construction Co., Bismarck, ND
1976– 1986	**Self-Employed**—home builder Pierre, SD
Prior:	Part-time laborer during high school; served apprenticeship as carpenter with Elmer D. Smith & Sons in Cheyenne, WY
Education:	
1975	**Cheyenne Sr. High School,** Cheyenne, WY
Other:	**Bismarck Technical School** Blueprint Reading and Estimating
Affiliations:	Carpenters' Union
Interests:	Hunting; fishing; gardening

(FOR AMPLIFICATION, SEE FOLLOWING.)

*Field where short-term employment listing need not be avoided. Project completion is an
acceptable reason for termination of employment. Basic skills shown through variety of jobs
satisfactorily completed. Range of supervisory capability demonstrated by cost of projects successfully completed.*

Amplified Resume:

Anthony J. Micelli
-Page 2-

EMPLOYMENT HIGHLIGHTS

June 1991–Present
J. Ackerman & Sons
Temporary position as carpenter while seeking supervisory position on construction project.

June 1989–Dec. 1990
Regal Homes, Inc.
General Superintendent of construction of the "Skyline" apartment house, a $4 million, four-floor, 90-apartment brick and block building with brick veneer.

Directed a total of 90 workers in all trades; directly supervised carpenters and masons. Personally supervised installation of storm and sanitary sewers, and subcontracted work in plumbing, electrical, steel, and heating. Purchased mason materials and carpenter requirements.

Results: Project completed four months ahead of schedule. No union disputes.

March 1988–May 1989
Hastings Contracting Company
General construction superintendent. Handled such projects as building remodeling, manhole construction, roads, and water lines. Supervised as many as four jobs simultaneously with varying numbers of workers according to project requirements.

Reason for leaving: Completion of projects.

Jan. 1987–Feb. 1988
Lindsay Construction Company
Construction Superintendent directing mason and carpentry work of up to 85 workers. Hired and laid off (through a foreperson) carpenters, masons, and laborers.

Results: $1 million apartment house completed 1 month ahead of schedule and under budget.

Reason for leaving: Company liquidation.

References on request.

Synopsis of Resume:

Sherman T. Conklin

542 Langley Road   **Great Falls, Montana 59401**   **(406) 781-8664**

Job Objective: General Contractor

Experience:
1989–Present   **General Contractor—Self-employed**
                      Conklin & Son Construction Company, Great Falls, MT

1986–89   **General Contractor—Self-employed**
                 Partnership, Casper, WY

1978–84   Miscellaneous employments in Cheyenne, WY:
                 milling machine operator, operator of heavy highway
                 equipment, mason, carpenter

Education:
1984–86   **Haxton Institute**, Olympia, WA
                 Full-time, two-year course in Building Construction.
                 Graduated third in a class of 47.

Other: •International Correspondence School
                    Architectural course

                    •Casper High School, Casper, WY
                    Adult education courses in Real Estate Appraisal,
                    Business Law, and Accounting

                    •Eastern Montana College of Education, Billings, MT
                    Advanced course for home builders

                    •Builders Management Seminars:
                    Olympia, WA; San Francisco, CA; Chicago, IL; New York, NY

Affiliations: Great Falls Home Builders Association

Will relocate within state.

(FOR AMPLIFICATION, SEE FOLLOWING.)

Continuing education cited in detail to impress potential employer with efforts to remain current in field.

Amplified Resume:

Sherman T. Conklin
-Page 2-

EMPLOYMENT HIGHLIGHTS

1991-Present
General Contractor. Build standard homes and small commercial buildings. Contracts range from $40,000 to $500,000. Services include sewer and water-line work, masonry, plumbing, carpentry, and painting.

Licensed real estate salesperson. Contact architects, brokers, finance officers of lending institutions, and prospective clients. Estimate consistently within 1% to 2%. Familiar with mortgage procedures, bank lending, real estate codes, and building codes. Up to ten projects underway simultaneously in different locations. Maintain a flow sheet of work progress indicating materials and money required at estimated times.

1990
Expanded own business to include small commercial, sewer, electrical and water-line work; building; carpentry; and masonry.

1989
Formed own business with family member, subcontracting for various developers. Had up to 50 employees on weekly payroll. Was construction superintendent for community center project.

1986–89
Formed partnership employing about 10 personnel to take painting contracts. Expanded to include mason and carpenter contracting. Sold out to partner at a profit.

Reason for change: Wish to work for established firm rather than operate own business.

References available.

Synopsis of Resume:

Stanley R. Moran

74 Atkins Street
Nashville, TN 37205
(615) 431-7651

Job Objective: Position in supervision on foreperson level, in charge of
punch press, grinding, or machine shop.

Experience:

1990–Present;   **ACE SIGNAL CORP.** (over 1,000 employees)
1987–88   12 Market Street, Nashville, TN
                  Foreperson of punch press, grinding, and gear cutting departments

1988–90   **GLEASON MANUFACTURING CO.** (500 employees)
                  300 West 50th Street, Knoxville, TN
                  Tool and die maker

Prior: Assistant manager of family-owned restaurant in Atlanta, GA;
                  left upon sale of restaurant.

Education: **Fulton Senior High School,** Atlanta, GA

Other: **Brewer Business Academy,** Atlanta, GA
                  Bookkeeping and Accounting courses
                  Winslow Technical Institute
                  Machine shop courses for apprenticeship
                  Tennessee Agricultural & Industrial State University
                  Courses included Drafting, Blueprint Reading,
                  Mathematics, Business Management, and Personnel
                  Management.

Interests: Hunting; fishing; softball

Will relocate for the right opportunity.

(FOR AMPLIFICATION, SEE FOLLOWING.)

Amplified as a one-employment record to point up solid background in field of present job objective.
Brief listing of former employments adequately fulfills purpose of showing steady work history.

Amplified Resume:

Stanley R. Moran
Page 2

EMPLOYMENT HIGHLIGHTS

1990–Present;
1987–88
ACE SIGNAL CORP.
Manufacturer of signals and air traffic/vehicular systems

Originally employed as tool crib attendant. Promoted to machinist. Promoted to tool and die maker. Promoted to Foreperson of the Punch Press Dept. with responsibility for fourteen operators, five-sheet metal workers, and three set-up workers. At different periods a second shift was added, giving authority over a maximum of approximately forty personnel.

Utilized heavy, medium, and light presses, working with steel, brass, bronze, silver, and other metals. Work ranged from pressing heavy metal for railroad equipment to small high-precision work for electrical devices.

During departmental reorganization, was given responsibility for Grinding Dept. (operation of cylindrical, rotary, and surface grinders) and Gear Cutting Dept. (gear cutting and broaching).

Interviewed, hired, and trained replacement personnel.

Results:

1. Work regularly completed on schedule
2. Low rejection record
3. Minimum of personnel problems brought to Grievance Committee
4. Minimum customer complaints

During further departmental reorganization, group was absorbed into Milling and Drilling Dept. under the direction of its Senior Foreperson.

Reason for desiring change: Desire position that will fully utilize training, ability, and managerial experience.

References available.

Synopsis of Resume:

PHILIP C. CONWELL
12 Kaiser Ave.
Boise, ID 83702
(208) 820-3001

JOB OBJECTIVE: Plant Manager

EXPERIENCE:
1987–Present   **GENERAL MANAGER**
Greer Manufacturing Co., Boise, ID
(Manufacturers of food handling equipment)

1984–87   **PRODUCTION CONTROL EXPEDITER**
Hadden Meter Company, Boise, ID (1,000 employees)
Resigned to accept offer from above company.

Prior: Summer employments during college period:
machine shop assistant, construction worker, etc.

EDUCATION:
1980–84   **MONTANA STATE UNIVERSITY**, Missoula, MT
B.S. in Business Administration

SERVICE:
1976–80   **U.S. NAVY.** Ensign: served as flight
instructor and aide to commanding officer.
Honorably discharged—no Reserve commitment.

INTERESTS: Hunting; fishing; golf

AFFILIATIONS: Chamber of Commerce; 1991–92 chairman of Boise Republicans

(FOR AMPLIFICATION, SEE FOLLOWING.)

Responsibilities of major employment classified to demonstrate ability to cope with wide range of problems involved in small plant managment. Major plant expediting (indicated by number of employess) important to well-rounded plant experience. However, as details of such work would be familiar to prospective employers in this field, they are omitted.

Amplified Resume:

Philip C. Conwell
- Page 2 -

EMPLOYMENT HIGHLIGHTS

1987–Present
GREER MANUFACTURING COMPANY

General Manager, promoted from Assistant General Manager.

Family-owned business specializes in complete packaging of potatoes, onions, and other produce for grocers. Center consists of graders, washers, conveyors, etc. Some combinations reach 75 feet in length with single installations selling in substantial five-figure sums. Other items are designed and produced to perform special operations. Plant fabrication includes steel and wood with complete shop facilities for both mediums.

Complete charge of plant and production. Hire, fire, and direct a continuing training program for new employees. Responsibilities extend beyond plant, including:

- **Sales**
  Assist dealers with customer contact; make direct sales.

- **Troubleshooting**
  Survey problem to be solved; make initial sketches, followed by actual design and layout; develop cost of components and fabrication; purchase required materials or components.

- **Supervision**
  Supervise construction and designate crew to follow shipment and assembly in purchasers' plants. Personally check operating problems and implement solutions.

- **Public Relations**
  Excellent labor relations with plant personnel. Maintain good customer relations despite communication difficulties related to lack of technical skills in most clients.

Result: Plant's profit volume has increased 20%.

Reason for desiring change: Have advanced to highest possible level in family-owned business; seek broader opportunity.

References available.

Synopsis of Resume:

ALICIA ECHEVARRIA
17 Orchard Place
Houston, TX 77006
(713) 514-7443

JOB OBJECTIVE: Production Control Manager

EXPERIENCE:
1986–August 1992   **PRODUCTION CONTROL SUPERINTENDENT**
Ames Lumber Products Corporation
Houston, TX

1982–86   **SENIOR STAFF CONSULTANT**
Swenson Management Advisory Consultants, Inc.
98 East 14th Street, Chicago Heights, IL

1977–82   **HEAD OF PLANNING**
(Promoted from machinist)
Clinton Machine Co.
Columbus, OH

EDUCATION:
1973–77   **Tiffin University**, Tiffin, OH
B.S. in Commerce
Financed approximately 50% of college expenses
Dean's List senior year

Other: **Clinton Machine Company,** San Francisco, CA
Yearly seminars in management and computer applications

AFFILIATIONS: American Production & Control Society; Chamber of Commerce

(FOR AMPLIFICATION, SEE FOLLOWING.)

Solid background presented through specifics of present position and general details of former positions. Reasons for leaving excellent position are of personal nature, better explained at interview.

Amplified Resume:

Alicia Echevarria
- Page 2 -

EMPLOYMENT HIGHLIGHTS

1986–August 1992
AMES LUMBER PRODUCTS CORP.
Production Control Manager with the specific assignment of establishing a three-plant unified corporate production control organization.

Established organization, tying in sales forecasts on stock and special orders, outside warehouse on nationwide basis, with proper stocks for prompt customer service, scheduling of production and shipments, and appropriate raw materials purchasing. Task complicated by rapid company growth (from three to six plants and individual plant company growth).

Promoted to Production Control Superintendent of headquarters plant in Houston. Department operates within a plant employing 900 workers with productive volume in substantial seven figures.

Directed a department of 110 workers in the following areas: scheduling, order processing, shipping, inventory control, receiving,warehousing, purchasing, and traffic.

Results:

1. Staff trained in corporate setup has taken over other plants; workers presently in training at Houston slated for department head positions.

2. All standards set by management have been met or exceeded; low turnover of personnel.

3. 20% salary increase, plus bonuses.

Reason for leaving: To be discussed at interview.

References available.

Synopsis of Resume:

Harold J. Beale

44 Holly Road
Salem, OR 97306
(503) 421-8753

Job Objective: Shop Supervision, Welding Foreperson, Instructor in Welding

Experience:

1988–Present   SPECIALTY WELDER, WELDER FOREPERSON
Cooper-Noonan, a division of Salem Steel, Inc.
Salem, OR

1983–88   SELF-EMPLOYED—owner of welding shop and welding school

Prior   Farm work during high school period

Education:

1983   MAKEY WELDING SCHOOL, Boise, ID
One-year welding course, included acetylene welding

1980   WOLF POINT HIGH SCHOOL, Wolf Point, MT

Other   I.C.S. Welding Course; varied safety and miscellaneous
company courses

Interests: Restoring antique cars; camping

(FOR AMPLIFICATION, SEE FOLLOWING.)

*Level of supervisory responsibility shown through number of
persons supervised; success of effort shown through promotion.*

Amplified Resume:

Harold J. Beale
- Page 2 -

EMPLOYMENT HIGHLIGHTS

1988–Present
COOPER-NOONAN, a division of Salem Steel, Inc.

Originally employed in Template Shop as helper; promoted to multiple punch helper; promoted to welder.

Promoted to Welding Inspector; served as sole plant inspector to 320 welders.

Promoted to Foreperson of approximately 50 welders in Marine Division of Salem Steel.

Appointed Navy Yard instructor for new welders. Appointed Welding Foreperson on Navy Yard outfitting docks. Returned to plant as Specialty Welder when Navy work slowed down.

Serve as Specialty and Acetylene welder. Collaborate with engineering department testing new varieties of welding materials; assist in deciding on recommended changes.

Reason for desiring change: Wish to transfer from steel industry.

Willing to relocate overseas.

Personal references available on request. Please do not contact present company until after interview.

Synopsis of Resume:

Gerald L. Maurer

76 Caldwell Street
Binghamton, NY 13903
(716) 643-3419

Job Objective: Tool Engineer or related position

Experience:
1986–Present   TOOL ENGINEER
Ansco, Binghamton, NY
(1,500 employees. Producers of color photographic film,
microfilm, copy papers, etc.)

1979–86   FOREPERSON (tool and die group)
Marx Tool & Gauge Co., Trenton, NJ
(Largest shop of kind on East Coast)

Education:
1978   **East High School,** Allentown, PA
Junior-year class president

Tool and Die Making Apprenticeship
Courses including blueprint reading

Special Skills: Moderate knowledge of German; some computer experience

Interests: Baseball; bowling; camping

Affiliations: American Legion

(FOR AMPLIFICATION, SEE FOLLOWING.)

*Despite lack of formal training, applicant demonstrates high degree of self-development, as
shown by level of responsibility and concrete dollars-and-cents results. Reason for leaving
cannot be briefly stated and will be discussed at interview.*

Amplified Resume:

Gerald L. Maurer
- Page 2 -

EMPLOYMENT HIGHLIGHTS

1986–Present
ANSCO

Tool Engineer
- Direct machine shop.
- Determine equipment required to handle foreseeable production.
- Develop cost of necessary equipment.
- Assist in preparation of drawings and data necessary for producing equipment within or without the plant.
- Cooperate with Quality Control to solve problems connected with production machinery.
- Improve existing production machinery to reduce maintenance or downtime.

Results:
1. Determined cause of rapid wear of German-made dies for punching track in film. Improved die life from 6 weeks to 11 months, resulting in substantial inventory savings.

2. Improved entire operation of film and paper-backing slitting machines, eliminating a loss of 3 cuts in every 30, and a second loss of 4 in 12 on second coating of same film, thereby compounding the savings on tens of thousands of film rolls daily.

3. Eliminated costly dies purchase by creation of fixture to make deckled-edge dies in company shop.

4. Conceived idea of recutting to smaller standard-size film which was formerly discarded for improper slitting. Supervised rework of machine (formerly used for different purpose). Savings have exceeded $2,500 monthly.

5. Revamped inoperative machines; accompanied major rejuvenation of production materials.

Reason for desiring change: To be discussed at interview.

References available.

Synopsis of Resume:

NICHOLAS A. ROCHE

78 Doyle St.
Trenton, NJ 08607
(609) 242-9003

JOB OBJECTIVE: Traffic Manager or Assistant

EXPERIENCE:
1987–Present   **ELECTRONIC DIVISION OF UNITED ELECTROCOM, INC.,**
                      Trenton, NJ
                      Senior Rate Clerk

1984–87   **ALLIED TRANSPORT COMPANY**, Perth Amboy, NJ
                      Assistant Terminal Manager

EDUCATION:
1991   **BRADEN INSTITUTE**, Trenton, NJ
                          Course in Traffic Management; graduated 1st in class

1984   **TRAFFIC MANAGERS INSTITUTE**, Perth Amboy, NJ
                          Course in ICC Law and Procedure

1983   **CARVER HIGH SCHOOL**, St. Paul, MN

INTERESTS: Do-it-yourself home projects; spectator sports

AFFILIATIONS: Transportation Club of Trenton; 1991 vice president of Little
                      League, Perth Amboy, NJ

(FOR AMPLIFICATION, SEE FOLLOWING.)

Amplified Resume:

Nicholas A. Roche
-Page 2-

EMPLOYMENT HIGHLIGHTS

1987–Present
ELECTRONICS DIVISION OF UNITED ELECTROCOM, INC.

1990
Senior Rate Clerk, assuming duties of Assistant Traffic Manager. Handle all technical matters within the department; attend meetings of the Traffic and Rate Committee. Familiar with all procedures, regulations, laws, and tariffs; perform some import and export work.

As a result of personal efforts, company has switched from rail to intercoastal shipping, resulting in 40% savings on sizable electronic component shipments.

1988
Senior Rate Clerk, assuming duties of Traffic Manager. Supervised personnel, gave assignments, made contacts with transportation companies, routed shipments, etc. Devised routing charts, revamped filing system, set up rate charts, and leveled distribution equitably among carriers to obtain exceptional shipping service.

1987
Junior Rate Clerk. Processed and audited freight bills; traced shipments; scheduled shipments from new warehouse at distance from plant. Ordered and scheduled trucks, routed shipments, and set up operations that were turned over to regular shipping group.

Reason for desiring change: Desire position utilizing on-the-job experience as well as recently completed advanced traffic management course.

1984–87
ALLIED TRANSPORT CO.

Employed as manifest clerk; promoted to Rate and Billing Clerk; promoted to Office Manager supervising previous work and clerks. Transferred to Trenton as Assistant Terminal Manager. Left to accept position above.

References available.

Synopsis of Resume:

ANN MARIE TURNER
4087 Helene Street
Sarasota, FL 33581
(813) 922-7980

JOB OBJECTIVE: Elementary School Teacher

EXPERIENCE:
1981–Present   SARASOTA COUNTY SCHOOLS, Sarasota, FL
                        Sixth-grade teacher

1978–81   UNIVERSITY OF MIAMI, Miami, FL
                        Laboratory technician

1972–78   COMMUNITY CONSOLIDATE SCHOOL DISTRICT,
                    Arlington Heights., IL
                        Sixth-grade science teacher

1968–70   WHITEHALL CITY SCHOOLS, Columbus, OH
                        Seventh-grade teacher

EDUCATION:
1982   LAVERNE COLLEGE, LaVerne, CA
                        Master's degree in Elementary Education

1968   OHIO STATE UNIVERSITY, Columbus, OH
                        B.S. in Education

Other: Ongoing workshops and seminars in science field

INTERESTS: Tennis; travel; swimming; needlework; reading

AFFILIATIONS: Ohio State University Alumni Association; PTA; National
                    Education Association; United Teaching Profession; Sarasota
                    County Teachers Association; Women's Network

Willing to relocate.

(FOR AMPLIFICATION, SEE FOLLOWING.)

Technique for consolidating pertinent job experience for present objective.

Amplified Resume:

Ann Marie Turner
Page 2

TEACHING EXPERIENCE

1981–Present
SARASOTA COUNTY SCHOOLS

1990   County changed to Middle School concept, eliminating sixth grade; returned to Sarasota Brookside School.

Teach as member of team consisting of three teachers responsible for approximately 90 students. Initially responsible for science subjects; in 1992 added language arts; presently teach both subjects during a seven-period day.

1983   Transferred to Venice, FL. Taught approximately 30 sixth-grade students in self-contained classroom. Subjects: math, language arts (spelling, reading, and English), social studies, and science.

1981   Instructor in experimental school trying new educational concepts. Responsible for mixed classroom of three grade levels, planning, teaching, guiding, and evaluating students.

Reason for desiring change: Wish to relocate to area with higher salary scale.

1978-1981
UNIVERSITY OF MIAMI, Miami, FL

Laboratory techinician at Veterans' Hospital, involved in drug research study for United Chemical Co. Duties included drawing and processing blood, assisting physician in patient examinations, maintaining patient records, handling correspondence, and attending autopsies. Left to return to teaching profession.

1968–78
OHIO AND ILLINOIS SCHOOLS

1972   Taught sixth-grade science at Junior. High level in Arlington, Illinois; left to relocate in Florida.

1968   Taught seventh grade at Whitehall City Schools; left to relocate to Illinois.

References available.

Synopsis of Resume:

LOUISE IKEDA
3 Woodthrush Drive
West Nyack, NY 10994
(914) 358-7917

JOB OBJECTIVE:	Social worker

EXPERIENCE:

1988–Present	ROCKLAND COMMUNITY HEALTH CENTER, Pamona, NY Field Placement
1983–88	ONTARIO COUNTY COUNSELING SERVICES, Canandaigua, NY Individual, marital, and family counseling
Prior	COMMUNITY SERVICE Member of two state commissions to oversee equality of care in state and nonprofit residential facility Board member and officer in human service agencies for advocacy and services

EDUCATION:

FORDHAM UNIVERSITY
GRADUATE SCHOOL OF SOCIAL SERVICE
Degrees: M.S.W.
Major: Services to individuals and families
Minor: Services to groups

ST. THOMAS COLLEGE, Sparkill, NY
Degree: B.A.
Major: English
Minor: Education

Other:	Certificate in Data Processing from Sparkhill Community College
INTERESTS:	Travel; handicrafts
AFFILIATIONS:	National Association of Social Workers; Association for Down's Syndrome Children; League of Women Voters

(FOR AMPLIFICATION, SEE FOLLOWING.)

Older applicant does not list years in which she received degrees to prevent prospective employer from determining her age or deciding that her educational qualifications are "outdated."

Amplified Resume:

Louise Ikeda
-Page 2-

EMPLOYMENT HIGHLIGHTS

1988–Present
ROCKLAND COMMUNITY HEALTH CENTER

Member of crisis intervention team whose responsibilities include short- and long-term treatment of adolescents and adults. Clients cover full range of diagnostic categories as well as wide socioeconomic backgrounds.

Additionally, co-therapist in weekly crisis intervention group handling variety of intra-psychic and personal problems. Duties include suicide/emergency hospitalization evaluations; diagnostic assessment; and periodic consultations with psychiatrists and community agencies.

Spearheading project to establish spouse and child abuse center and support team.

Reason for desiring change: Wish to broaden experience outside of crisis intervention.

1983–88
ONTARIO COUNTY COUNSELING SERVICES

Perform individual, marital, and family counseling, including diagnostic assessment, upon referrrals from family court, probation department, and community agencies.

In 1985, added responsibility for screening and training new volunteer counselors. Assumed public relations duties; addressed community organizations to increase public awareness of programs and to recruit volunteers.

Reason for leaving: To accept offer above.

References on request.

Synopsis of Resume:

LINDA SOBEL
159 Antlers Drive
Duluth, MN 55802
(218) 643-4962

JOB OBJECTIVE: Patent Attorney

EXPERIENCE:
1988–Present   PATENT ATTORNEY (Associate)
                    Armstron & McKenzie, Patent Attorneys
                    Duluth, MN

1984–88   PATENT ATTORNEY
                    Bigelow Manufacuring Co., a division of General Bronze Corp.
                    Pittsburgh, PA

1983–84   PATENT ENGINEER
                    General Electric Co., Washington, D.C.

1978–83   PRIVATE LAW PRACTICE
                    Philadelphia, PA

EDUCATION:

1977   **Georgetown University,** Washington, D.C.
                    L.L.B.

Certification: Admitted to Bar, State of Pennsylvania, 1978
                    Member Minnesota State Bar
                    Admission to practice before U.S. Patent Office, U.S. Court of
                        Customs and Patent Appeals, U.S. Court of Claims, and U.S.
                        Supreme Court

INTERESTS: Chess; golf; spectator sports

                    (FOR AMPLIFICATION, SEE FOLLOWING.)

This resume stresses certification and experience to whet prospective employer's interest.

Amplified Resume:

Linda Sobel
-Page 2-

EMPLOYMENT HIGHLIGHTS

1988–Present
ARMSTRON & MCKENZIE
Patent Attorneys

Prepare and prosecute patent applications; advise and render opinions on infringement questions and related matters.

Reason for desiring change: Seek industrial connection, preferably in New England area; income commensurate with experience and ability.

1984–88
BIGELOW MANUFACTURING CO., a division of General Bronze Corp.

Patent attorney. Prepared and prosecuted patent applications covering the electrical and electromechanical arts.

Accepted above post to gain experience in infringement, licensing, and litigations.

1983–84
GENERAL ELECTRIC CO.

Patent Engineer in Washington, D.C. office. Admitted to practice before the U.S. Patent Office.

Relocated to Pennsylvania due to family obligations.

1978–83
PRIVATE PRACTICE

Private law practice incorporating **commercial practice, contract matters, real estate, receiverships,** and **bankruptcy.** Formed various corporations; served as corporate officer. Clerk of Mortgage and Real Estate Committee for the Assembly in the Pennsylvania State Legislature.

Relocated to Washington, D.C. to specialize in patent law.

References available.

Synopsis of Resume:

SARAH RYAN
303 Lawton Road
Orlando, FL 32803
(305) 423-5316

JOB OBJECTIVE: Legal Assistant/Paralegal in private law firm

EXPERIENCE:
1990–Present   PUBLIC DEFENDER
                   Orlando, Florida
                     Investigator

EDUCATION:
1988–90   MANATEE JUNIOR COLLEGE, Bradenton, Florida
              Associate of Science Degree in Legal Assistant Program
              Courses included Accounting, Economics, Written Communica-
              tions, Government, Human Relations, Law Office Management
              and Procedures, Legal Terminology Research, Real Property
              Law, Wills, Trusts and Probate, Principles of Family Law, Civil
              Criminal Procedures, General Law, Introduction to Litigation
              and Evidence, Criminal Law

INTERESTS: Spectator sports; sailing; reading

AFFILIATIONS: Member National Association of Legal Assistants, Inc.
                        Member Orlando Sailing Club

(FOR AMPLIFICATION, SEE FOLLOWING.)

Older applicant decided to pursue a lifelong interest in law. Her resume focuses stricly on the legal aspect of her education and experience; she does not list her past, disparate employments, such as apartment complex manager and supervisor of a bank's mortgage loan department. No chronological gap between graduation and first paralegal position; prospective employer may well forego questioning about experience prior to 1988.

Amplified Resume:

Sarah Ryan
-Page 2-

EMPLOYMENT HIGHLIGHTS

1990–Present

Investigator, hired three months after commencing unsalaried internship with Public Defender.

Handle Juvenile and Misdemeanor investigations as well as overflow of felony cases.

Interview incarcerated defendants and assist them in obtaining reasonable bonds. Interview persons being held in Juvenile Detention for daily hearings.

Assist "walk-ins" needing help and advice on a court proceeding as well as general information pertaining to the processes involved in obtaining a public defender (prior to arraignment).

Interview witnesses, arrange for photographs, make all diagrams, and tabulate any related evidence for use in ultimate defense. Evaluate and coordinate all evidence and information for discussion with attorneys.

Maintain good public relations with all other governmental agencies involved in the Criminal Justice System, as well as the lawyers and co-workers in Public Defender's employ.

Attend professional seminars to keep abreast of new methods, procedures, and general updating to aid and improve job performance.

Reason for desiring change: Seek position with private law firm; salary commensurate with responsibilities and experience.

References available. Please do not contact present employer at this time.

Synopsis of Resume:

PETER BRANT
890 Maple Avenue
Irvine, CA 92714
(714) 334-8973

OBJECTIVE:	Travel Agent/Consultant

EXPERIENCE:

1990–92	WORLEY TRAVEL AGENCY, Los Angeles, CA **Travel Consultant**
1983–90	LOS ANGELES COUNTY, Los Angeles, CA **Social Worker**
1982–83	**Personal travel:** Africa, China, Mexico

EDUCATION:

1989–90	LOS ANGELES CITY COLLEGE **Travel Agent Course**
1978–83	BENNINGTON COLLEGE, Bennington, VT **Degree:** B.A. **Major:** Psychology
Current	INSTITUTE OF CERTIFIED TRAVEL AGENTS Enrolled in **Certified Travel Counselor** course given on seminar basis. Covers business, personnel, marketing, and travel. Geared toward pursuit of excellence and professionalism in the travel field.

INTERESTS:	Raising dogs; gardening
AFFILIATIONS:	Junior League; Individual Travel Agents

Free to relocate.

(FOR AMPLIFICATION, SEE FOLLOWING.)

Amplified Resume:

Peter Brant
-Page 2-

EMPLOYMENT HIGHLIGHTS

1990–92
WORLEY TRAVEL AGENCY

Full-time travel consultant, promoted from trainee, in eight-member agency catering to affluent, knowledgeable clientele.

Consulted and advised clients in trip planning; made computerized airline reservations; phoned for land, rail, hotel, and car reservations. Collected payments; paid suppliers; followed up on final documents and details, as well as problems and complaints.

Made periodic, expense-paid trips to check hotel, ship, and accommodations in general, in advance of recommendation to clients.

Destinations have included Spain, Russia, Alaska, and the Caribbean Islands.

1983–90
LOS ANGELES COUNTY

Employed as social worker in the Aid to the Disabled branch of very large agency. Interviewed over 300 families per year, computing their welfare budgets based on need. Promoted to assistant medical social worker working with the elderly and disabled.

Reason for leaving: Career move into travel industry.

References on request.

Synopsis of Resume:

WENDY WAINWRIGHT
307 Copperwood Court
Colleyville, TX 76034
(817) 987-5602

OBJECTIVE: Airline Flight Attendant

EXPERIENCE: **SOUTHERN AIRLINES**, Miami, FL
1989–92   Flight attendant, promoted from reservations agent.
                      Relocated to Texas.

Prior   **GIRL SCOUTS OF AMERICA**
                      Summer employment during high school and college:
                      Water Safety Instructor and Waterfront Director

EDUCATION:
1986–88   **KATHERINE GIBBS SCHOOL**, New York, NY
                      Secretarial and business courses

SKILLS: Typing; computer knowledge

LANGUAGES: Fluent Spanish; working knowledge of French

INTERESTS: Aerobics; swimming; classical music

Free to relocate anywhere in the United States.

(FOR AMPLIFICATION, SEE FOLLOWING.)

Note: To slant resume to a specific airline, call the local office and ask for address to write for brochure listing qualifications and application blank. Major airlines are cooperative and happy to oblige with information on all available positions and requirements. Some positions at airlines, other than Flight Attendant, include Customer Service Agent; Clerk-Typist; General Clerical; Reservation Sales Agent; Customer Service Support Agent; and Maintenance Utility Employee.

Amplified Resume:

Wendy Wainwright
-Page 2-

EMPLOYMENT HIGHLIGHTS

1989–92
SOUTHERN AIRLINES

Reservations sales agent assigned to the Miami, FL office; trained in airline computer operation and telephone sales.

Transferred to Flight Attendant school, covering:

- Technical and operational instruction
- Customer service orientation
- Safety
- Security
- Emergency procedures
- Infant care
- Swift food/beverage service procedures

Assigned to Flight Attendant base station in Miami; flew approximately 70 hours each month. Excellent record of attendance and fulfillment of assigned duties; given performance rating of "Above Average," plus periodic salary raises.

Reason for leaving: Relocation to Texas.

References on request.

Part 3

Occupational Outlook 2000

EMPLOYMENT PROJECTIONS FOR THE NINETIES*

The U.S. economy is projected to add 18 million new jobs by the year 2000. Over half of these jobs are expected to be in service-producing industries, with the greatest number in health, retail trade, and business services.

The Fastest-Growing Occupations

Table 1 shows that half of the twenty occupations with the fastest projected growth rates are health-related occupations. Of these the job of medical assistant will grow most rapidly, followed by that of home health aide. Because of new technologies, patients are likely to undergo more tests, more diagnostic procedures and more aggressive treatments, thus greatly increasing the need for radiologic technicians and technologists, medical record technicians, medical secretaries, physical therapists, surgical technologists, physical and corrective therapy assistants and aides, and occupationsl therapists.

High growth is also expected for occupations related to the continuing spread of computer technology. The number of data processing equipment repairers should increase rapidly to maintain the growing stock of computer and related equipment. Growth of operations research analysts is also expected. These workers perform data analyses of the operations of manufacturing and other business organizations in order to improve efficiency. Computer systems analysts and computer programmers will be needed to improve methods of satisfying the expanding data processing needs of organizations.

Another fast-growing industry within business services is temporary help supply. Employers find temporary help advantageous because of the ease and convenience of meeting peak workloads or covering for absent permanent employees. Also, because temporary help supply agencies typically provide fewer benefits, their rates frequently are competitive with the cost of directly hiring additional employees. Workers are attracted to these agencies because of the training opportunities and the flexible scheduling offered. Industry experts expect the skill level of temporary help workers to shift, with a slight increase in the proportion of computer programmers, accountants, engineers, and computer-skilled clerical workers, and a slight decline in the proportion of laborers and clerical jobs that are not computer related.

Other growth occupations include securities and financial services sales representatives, travel agents, and social welfare service aides.

Adapted from Outlook 2000, U.S. Department of Labor, Bureau of Labor Statistics.

Table 1. Fastest growing occupations, 1988–2000

[Numbers in thousands]

Occupation	Employment		Numerical change	Percent change
	1988	2000		
Paralegals	83	145	62	75.3
Medical assistants	149	253	104	70.0
Home health aides	236	397	160	87.9
Radiologic technologists and technicians	132	218	87	66.0
Data processing equipment repairers	71	115	44	61.2
Medical records technicians	47	75	28	59.9
Medical secretaries	207	327	120	58.0
Physical therapists	68	107	39	57.0
Surgical technologists	35	55	20	58.4
Operations research analysts	55	85	30	55.5
Securities and financial services sales workers . .	200	309	109	54.8
Travel agents	142	219	77	54.8
Computer systems analysts	403	617	214	53.5
Physical and corrective therapy assistants	39	60	21	52.5
Social welfare service aides	91	138	47	51.5
Occupational therapists	33	48	16	48.8
Computer programmers	519	769	250	48.1
Human services workers	118	171	53	44.9
Respiratory therapists	56	79	23	41.4
Correction officers and jailers	186	262	76	40.8

Occupations with the Largest Job Growth

In addition to rapidly growing occupations, those having the largest numerical increases are important in identifying careers that will provide favorable job opportunities. All of the occupations in Table 2 are among the largest in employment size. Employment size is a major factor in the number of openings that will occur, because of the need to replace workers who leave the labor force or transfer to other occupations. The industries with the projected greatest number of job openings are health services, retail trade, and educational services.

The retail trade industry is projected to have the highest growth because of an increasing demand for salespersons. The growing number of eating and drinking establishments have 3 of the top 20 occupations with the largest growth: waiters and waitresses; food counter, fountain, and related workers; and food preparation workers. Another retail trade occupation with a projected large increase is cashiers.

Registered nurses are expected to have the second highest increase in employment opportunities. Nursing aides and licensed practical nurses are two other high growth health occupations.

Education will be another growth industry during the next ten years. Most of the new jobs will be in the public sector, reflecting rising enrollment projected for elementary and secondary schools. The greatest increases will be for teachers, but teacher aides, counselors, technicians, and administrative staff will also see growth.

Other occupations that are expected to have large job gains are not as identifiable with an industry group and exhibit a wide range of skills and earnings levels. Janitors and cleaners, including maids and housekeeping cleaners lead this group. General managers and top executives are also projected to have increases because of the growing complexity of industrial and commercial organizations.

Table 2. Occupations with the largest job growth, 1988–2000
[Numbers in thousands]

Occupation	Employment		Numerical change	Percent change
	1988	2000		
Salesperson, retail...............................	3,834	4,564	730	19.0
Registered nurses	1,577	2,190	613	38.8
Janitors and cleaners, including maids and housekeeping cleaners........................	2,895	3,450	556	19.2
Waiters and waitresses	1,786	2,337	551	30.9
General managers and top executives...........	3,030	3,509	479	15.8
General office clerks............................	2,519	2,974	456	18.1
Services, except legal and medical	2,903	3,288	385	13.2
Nursing aides, orderlies, and attendants	1,184	1,562	378	31.9
Truck drivers, light and heavy	2,399	2,768	369	15.4
Receptionists and information clerks	833	1,164	331	39.8
Cashiers	2,310	2,614	304	13.2
Guards..	795	1,050	256	32.2
Computer programmers.........................	519	769	250	48.1
Food counter, fountain, and related	1,626	1,866	240	14.7
Food preparation workers	1,027	1,260	234	22.8
Licensed practical nurses	526	855	229	36.6
Teachers, secondary school	1,164	1,388	224	19.2
Computer systems analysts.....................	403	617	214	55.3
Accountants and auditors	963	1,174	211	22.0
Teachers, kindergarten and elementary.........	1,359	1,567	208	15.3

Expected Changes in Various Occupations

Occupation	Projected changes and reasons
Small increase	
Biological scientists	Small increase due to the expected increase in research and development (R&D) funds for biological and medical research. A moderate decrease is expected in miscellaneous business services because the demand for services provided by other workers in this industry is growing more rapidly than demand for services provided by this occupation.
Busdrivers, school	Small increase in education, public and private, due to the continuing shift of school-age population from cities to suburbs, resulting in an increased demand for school busing.
Camera and photographic equipment repairers	Small increase due to the introduction of new lines of technologically advanced equipment that will require service and repair.
Cooks, restaurant	Small increase in eating and drinking places as full-service restaurants increase more rapidly than fast-food restaurants.
Cost estimators	Small increase due to the increasing importance of cost estimation due to competitive and cost-cutting pressures.
Dentists	Small increase due to the trend toward group practices, which permit more efficient use of support staff.
Dining room and cafeteria attendants and bartender helpers	Small increase in eating and drinking places as other industries contract out food services, shifting employment from those industries into eating and drinking places.
Economists	Small increase because more economic research will occur as businesses strive to meet growing competition. A small decrease is expected in miscellaneous business services because the demand for services provided by other workers in this industry is growing more rapidly than demand for services provided by this occupation. No change is expected in government because the demand for economists in this sector is not expected to keep pace with other industries due to cutbacks in government expenditures.
Electricians	Small increase in electrical contractors due to the increasing use of automation and computers in manufacturing, which is expected to increase demand for electrical services.
Electronics repairers, commercial and industrial equipment	Small increase reflecting a greater use of electronic equipment.
Flight attendants	Small increase because little productivity improvement is expected due to regulations requiring 1 attendant per 50 passengers.
Gardeners and groundskeepers, except farm	Small increase in agricultural services due to more landscaping around commercial and residential buildings and greater use of lawn maintenance services.
Hosts and hostesses, restaurant/lounge/coffee shop	Small increase in eating and drinking places due to the employment growth in full-service restaurants and the growth of chain restaurants.
Insurance adjusters, examiners, and investigators	Small increase due to the growing complexity of the claims handled by adjusters.
Locomotive engineers	Small increase because engineers are little affected by technological change among railroad occupations, thus increasing their relative share of employment.
Machinists	Small increase because the work many machinists perform, especially that of maintenance machinists, is not easily automated.
Marketing, advertising, and public relations managers	Small increase reflecting the demands of an increasingly competitive economy.
Mining engineers, including mine safety engineers	Small increase in mining industries due to the relative revival of these industries and the subsequent need for new mining design.
Nursery workers	Small increase in crops, livestock, and livestock products due to the expected growth of the horticultural specialties sector, where most of these workers are concentrated. The same holds true for agricultural services and for retail nurseries and lawn and garden stores.
Occupational therapy assistants and aides	Small increase in hospitals reflecting anticipated increases in outpatient services.
Optical goods workers, precision	Small increase in used merchandise and retail stores, not elsewhere classified, due to the advent of vision care stores in which glasses are made on the premises. A small increase is also expected in optical and ophthalmic products because of the development of new optical technology and the expanding population of middle-aged and elderly individuals who require increased eyecare.

Expected Changes in Various Occupations

Occupation	Projected changes and reasons
Personnel, training, and labor relations managers and specialists	Small increase due to reglatory legislation, resulting in more numerous and complex labor relations; and more sophisticated training and development activities.
Pharmacists	Small increase in drug stores and proprietary stores due to the growing use of part-time pharmacists and an increase in the number of pharmacies offering services on a 24-hour basis. A moderate increase is expected in hospitals due to development of new drug therapies.
Rail yard engineers, dinkey operators, and hostlers	Small increase because engineers are little affected by technological change among railroad occupations, thus increasing their relative share of employment.
Registered nurses	Small increase in hospitals. Hospitals are delivering more complex care, requiring highly trained registered nurses in place of licensed practical nurses and nursing aides.
Science and mathematics technicians	Small increase reflecting the expected increase in R&D expenditures.
Social workers	Small increase in State and local government due to the expected growth of public welfare and health agencies which provide services to the elderly, mentally ill, and developmentally disabled.
Statisticians	Small increase because of the increasing application of statistical techniques to improve quality control and to counter foreign competition.
Teachers, secondary school	Small increase in educational services because enrollment in secondary schools is expected to increase as a proportion of total enrollment in educational services.
Tool and die makers	Small increase because of the continuing use of tools and dies in the production of plastic, ceramic, and composite parts.
Waiters and waitresses	Small increase in eating and drinking places resulting from employment growth in coffee shops and full-service restaurants, where this occupation is concentrated.
Moderate increase	
Administrative services managers	Moderate increase is expected to occur in the private sector as cost pressures require more efficient operations.
Advertising clerks	Moderate increase in newspapers due to the increasing importance of classified advertising for newspaper revenue.
Agricultural and food scientists	Moderate increase because research opportunities created by biotechnology will make more R&D funds available. A small increase is expected in miscellaneous business services because the demand for services provided by other workers in this industry is not growing as rapidly as demand for services provided by this occupation.
Air traffic controllers	Moderate increase due to the Federal Aviation Administration's plans to increase employment.
Automotive body and related repairers	Moderate increase in automobile repair shops due to declining productivity in collision repairs as automobiles become more difficult to repair.
Camera operators	Moderate increase due to the development and growing use of television minicameras.
Chemical engineers	Moderate increase due to the expected increase in R&D expenditures.
Chemists	Moderate increase due to expected increases in R&D funds. A small decrease is expected in miscellaneous business services because the demand for services provided by other workers in this industry is growing more rapidly than demand for services provided by this occupation.
Claims examiners, property and casualty insurance	Moderate increase in fire, marine, and casualty insurance due to the increasing complexity of marine insurance policies which is expanding the requirements for claims examining. A small increase is also expected in insurance agents, brokers, and services.
Combination machine tool setters, set-up operators, operators, and tenders	Moderate increase due to changing management practices and decreased unionization, which should result in a more flexible work force. These workers will increasingly be able to tend more than one type of machine, thus increasing the demand for their services.
Construction managers	Moderate increase due to the increasing complexity of construction projects, construction materials, and management techniques as well as the proliferation of regulations concerning zoning and building codes to meet energy, environmental, and other governmental requirements.

Expected Changes in Various Occupations

Occupation	Projected changes and reasons
Counselors	Moderate increase in educational services, public and private, as the role of counselors is being gradually expanded beyond academic counseling into such areas as family relations and substance abuse.
Court clerks	Moderate increase reflecting an increased concern about law and order, as well as efforts to reduce backlogs of cases.
Dectectives and investigators, except public protective service workers	Moderate increase in miscellaneous business services due to an increasing concern for personal safety and property and an increase in litigation, contributing to an increase in demand for investigators. Growth will be concentrated in the detective and investigative agencies which provide services on a contract basis.
Electroencephalographic technologists	Moderate increase in hospitals due to the use of technologists in new areas of neurodiagnostic testing such as surgical monitoring, evoked potential, sleep tracing, and brain mapping.
Electromedical and biomedical equipment repairers	Moderate increase in hospitals as they use more, and increasingly sophisticated, equipment.
Engineering, mathematics, and natural science managers	Moderate increase due to the expected increase in R&D expenditures. A small increase is expected in miscellaneous business services and engineering and architectural services because the demand for services provided by other workers in this industry is not growing as rapidly as demand for services provided by this occupation.
Food service and lodging managers	Moderate increase in eating and drinking places because the growth of chain restaurants will require more wage and salary managers and fewer self-employed managers. The same holds true for hotels and other lodging places because of the trend toward more chain-affiliated hotels.
Geologists, geophysicists, and oceanographers	Moderate increase resulting from the need to increase exploration for oil and other minerals.
Guards	Moderate increase in miscellaneous business services due to the growth in guard and security agencies that provide guards on a contract basis. Contract security firms have been growing rapidly because contracting out is easier and less expensive than operating an in-house security staff.
Human services workers	Moderate increase in State and local governments because public welfare and health agencies, which provide services to the elderly, mentally ill, and developmentally disabled are expected to continue to grow faster than other local and State agencies.
Industrial engineers, except safety engineers	Moderate increase reflecting the need to incorporate increasingly sophisticated production methods, such as robots and computers, into production systems. A small increase is expected in miscellaneous business services because the demand for services provided by other workers in this industry is not growing as rapidly as demand for services provided by this occupation.
Industrial machinery mechanics	Moderate increase reflecting an expected increase in the use of machinery in industry.
Industrial production managers	Moderate increase because expected increases in production will require increased managerial input.
Inspectors and compliance officers, except construction	Moderate increase in Federal and local governments due to increased activity in enforcement of environmental and other regulations. A small decrease in State government because some State activities are being undertaken by local government.
Judges, magistrates, and other judicial workers	Moderate increase in State government and a small increase in local government reflecting an increasing concern about law and order as well as efforts to reduce backlogs of cases waiting to be heard.
Lawyers	Moderate increase in industries other than legal services reflecting the trend toward doing more legal work in-house in order to control legal costs. Moderate increase expected in legal services to offset the declining ratios for secretaries, typists, and word processors stemming from increased computerization and automation of document preparation.
Log handling equipment operators	Moderate increase because of the continued improvement of mechanized operations which will displace manual operations, such as felling and bucking.
Manicurists	Moderate increase because the demand for services provided by other workers in the cosmetology industry is not growing as fast as the demand for manicurist services.
Meat, poultry, and fish cutters and trimmers, hand	Moderate increase in meat products because more meatcutting is being done by this occupation and less by more highly skilled butchers and meatcutters.

Expected Changes in Various Occupations

Occupation	Projected changes and reasons
Mechanical engineers	Moderate increase due to the need for more automated production systems and the expected increase in R&D expenditures. A small decrease is expected in miscellaneous business services because the demand for services provided by other workers in this industry is growing more rapidly than demand for services provided by this occupation.
Metallurgists and metallurgical, ceramic, and materials engineers	Moderate increase due to the expected increase in R&D expenditures. A moderate decrease is expected in miscellaneous business services because the demand for services provided by other workers in this industry is growing more rapidly than demand for services provided by this occupation.
Numerical-control machine tool operators and tenders, metal and plastic	Moderate increase because the use of numerically controlled machine tools has increased as they have become more refined and affordable.
Occupational therapists	Moderate increase in hospitals reflecting anticipated increases in outpatient services. A small increase in education due to expanded coverage of therapy services to school-age children.
Offset lithographic press operators	Moderate increase in newspapers and commercial printing and business forms due to the replacement of older letterpress technology.
Opticians, dispensing and measuring	Moderate increase in used merchandise and retail stores, not elsewhere classified, because demand for services provided by other occupations in this industry is not growing as fast as the demand for optical services. A significant decrease is expected in offices of "other health practitioners" as more optometrists form group practices.
Petroleum engineers	Moderate increase to offest declining ratios for other occupations in industries which employ petroleum engineers.
Pharmacy assistants	Moderate increase in hospitals as inpatients have more serious ailments and require more medication.
Photographers	Moderate increase in newspapers as newspapers require more photographs to fill the growing number of specialty and local sections.
Physical therapists	Moderate increase expected in hospitals reflecting an anticipated increase in demand for physical therapy services, particularly in outpatient services. Moderate increase also expected in offices of "other health practitioners," reflecting the trend of physical therapists to set up their own private practices. Consequently, a moderate decrease is expected in physicians' offices.
Physicists and astronomers	Moderate increase due to an expected growth in R&D funds. A significant decrease is expected in miscellaneous business services because the demand for services provided by other workers in this industry is growing more rapidly than demand for services provided by this occupation.
Property and real estate managers	Moderate increase in the real estate agents and managers industry due to growth in professional management of commercial and residential properties, condominiums, and community associations.
Radiologic technologists and technicians	Moderate increase in hospitals due to the growing use of noninvasive diagnostic techniques and technological advances. A significant increase is expected in offices of physicians because of an expected increase in the use of radiologic examinations, due to technological advances, positive impact on revenues, and growth in the number of group practices.
Respiratory therapists	Moderate increase in hospitals due to the growth of the elderly population, who traditionally have chronic lung and cardiopulmonary problems.
Securities and financial services sales workers	Moderate increase due to the growing array and compexity of financial products and the expansion of banks and financial institutions into other areas of financial services and products.
Typesetting and composing machine operators and tenders	Moderate increase in commercial printing and business forms and printing trade services due to these industries' ability to quickly adopt technology, enabling them to capture new adverising markets. A moderate decrease is expected in newspapers because of the decreased demand for typesetters and compositors arising from developments in computer technology such as electronic page makeup.
Underwriters	Moderate increase as the underwriting function becomes more important because of cost pressures.
Significant increase	
Actuaries	Significant increase because: 1) policies are increasing in number and complexity, reflecting the need for more comprehensive coverage; 2) the growth in activities relating to investment portfolios; and 3) the emergence of new insurance mechanisms, such as self-insurance.

Expected Changes in Various Occupations

Occupation	Projected changes and reasons
Bakers, bread and pastry	Significant increase in grocery stores as they continue to expand the range of products and services offered to customers. Moderate increase in eating and drinking places because full-service restaurants increasingly offer patrons breads, pastries, and other baked goods freshly baked on the premises.
Computer programmers	Significant increase due to the growing use of computers as improvements to software and hardware make computers more versatile and cheaper to use. Significant increase is also expected in telephone communications since the trend towards digital telephone networks means more software will be needed to run the system. No change is expected in the Federal Government due to its practice of contracting out programming services.
Computer systems analysts	Significant increase because improvements in hardware and software have resulted in computers which are cheaper and easier to use. With the increasing number of computer applications, more systems analysts will be needed to integrate various components into coherent systems. No change is expected in the Federal Government due to its tendency to contract out computer services.
Correction officers and jailers	Significant increase in Federal, State, and local governments because of growing concern about crime and the construction of new correctional facilities.
Data processing equipment repairers	Significant increase in wholesale trade and machinery and equipment and a moderate increase in computer and data processing services due to the growing use of computers as improvements to hardware and software make computers more versatile, cheaper, and easier to use.
Electrical and electronics engineers	Significant increase due to the increasing pace of innovation and the growing importance of electronics in many industries. No change is expected in miscellaneous business services because these workers are concentrated in R&D laboratories, which will grow more slowly than the rest of the industry.
Electrical and electronics technicians and technologists	Significant increase because the pace of innovation in electrical devices will accelerate and electronics will become more important in many industries. Small increase expected in miscellaneous business services because the demand for services provided by other workers in this industry is not growing as rapidly as demand for services provided by this occupation.
Farm managers	Significant increase in crops, livestock, and livestock products due to the increasing complexity of farming practices resulting from technological and competitive pressures.
Management analysts and consultants	Significant increase in miscellaneous business services due to the rapid growth of consulting and accounting firms, where most of these workers are concentrated.
Medical record technicians	Significant increase in hospitals due to changing reimbursement policies that require very precise and accurate coding.
Meteorologists	Significant increase in the Federal Government due to the National Weather Service's plans to hire additional meteorologists.
Millwrights	Significant increase due to expected increases in the amount of machinery needing installation by millwrights.
Operations research analysts	Significant increase as businesses attempt to develop more efficient operations.
Paralegals	Significant increase in legal services and a moderate increase in government due to the increasing role of this occupation as useful and effective members of the legal services team.
Photographic process workers, precision	Significant increase in mailing, reproduction, and commercial art reflecting the greater incorporation of photographs into commercial advertising copy. A moderate decrease is expected in miscellaneous business services because the demand for services provided by this occupation is growing at a slower rate than the demand for services provided by other occupations in this industry.
Programmers, numerical, tool, and process control	Significant increase reflecting the increased use of numerically controlled machine tools.
Shoe and leather workers and repairers	Significant increase in footwear, except rubber and plastic, due to greater numbers of older people who are more likely to have foot problems, requiring custom-made shoes. Also, since these workers do custom work, they are not affected by imports, as are other workers in this industry.
Subway and streetcar operators	Significant increase in local and suburban transportation, local government, and State government as more cities install new subway systems or add to existing lines.

Expected Changes in Various Occupations

Occupation	Projected changes and reasons
Surgical technologists	Significant increase in hospitals reflecting an increase in inpatient and outpatient surgery.
Small decrease	
Bank tellers	Small decrease due to the growing use of automated teller machines, terminals, and other electronic equipment for funds transactions.
Bookbinders	Small decrease due to the advent of new machinery which is capable of performing many bindery tasks in sequence, thus reducing the need for these workers.
Butchers and meatcutters	Small decrease because more meatcutting is being done by lesser skilled meat, poultry, and fish cutters rather than butchers and meatcutters.
Cannery workers	Small decrease due to continuing automation and resulting productivity increases.
Cashiers	Small decrease due to the increased use of bar code readers and scanners, which increases productivity.
Coil winders, tapers, and finishers	Small decrease due to continuing automation and resulting productivity increases.
Cooks, institution or cafeteria	Small decrease in education, public and private, since more food service functions in this industry are expected to be contracted out to the eating and drinking places industry in an effort to reduce costs. A moderate decrease is expected in nursing and residential care facilities, hospitals, and government for the same reason.
Drafters	Small decrease as computer-aided drafting technology is expected to make drafters more productive.
Electrolytic plating machine operators and tenders, setters, and set-up operators, metal and plastic	Small decrease due to the increased use of computer and numerically controlled machine tools and robotics, which increase operator productivity.
Fitters, structural metal, precision	Small decrease due to the development of new technologies and robotics, which will increase productivity.
Freight, stock, and material movers, hand	Small decrease due to improved material handling equipment. A significant decrease is expected in miscellaneous business services and personnel supply services because the demand for services provided by other workers in this industry is growing more rapidly than demand for services provided by this occupation.
Heaters, metal and plastic	Small decrease due to the continuing use of automated equipment, especially in the steel industry.
Heat treating machine operators and tenders, metal and plastic	Small decrease due to the growing use of automated equipment.
Industrial truck and tractor operators	Small decrease reflecting the increased use of automated material handling equipment in warehouses and factories.
Inspectors, testers, and graders	Small decrease due to the development of automated inspecting equipment, limiting the number of inspectors needed to check output. Also a factor is the growing emphasis on preventing defects before they occur by making production workers responsible for their own output.
Insurance claims clerks	Small decrease due to the spread of office automation in the form of word processing equipment and personal computers throughout the insurance industry.
Insurance policy processing clerks	Small decrease due to continuing office automation and resulting productivity increases.
Interviewing clerks, except personnel and welfare	Small decrease expected in hospitals, public and private, due to cost-cutting measures increasingly being taken by hospitals.
Janitors and cleaners	Small decrease in all industries, except services to dwellings and other buildings, due to the continuing practice of contracting out janitorial services.
Legal secretaries	Small decrease in legal services due to the trend toward paralegals taking over some of the job duties previously performed by secretaries.
Licensed practical nurses	Small decrease in hospitals. Hospitals are delivering more complex care, requiring highly trained registered nurses in place of licensed practical nurses. Small increase expected in nursing homes based on regulations requiring more licensed nurses.
Machine tool cutting operators and tenders, metal and plastic	Small decrease due to the greater use of computer-controlled equipment.

Expected Changes in Various Occupations

Occupation	Projected changes and reasons
Metal fabricators, structural metal products	Small decrease in fabricated structural metal products due to advances in factory automation and increased use of computer-controlled machinery and equipment.
Mining, quarrying, and tunneling occupations	Small decrease due to the expected development of more productive and larger capacity mining, quarrying, and tunneling machinery and equipment, making these workers more productive.
Nonelectrolytic plating machine operators and tenders, setters, and set-up operators, metal and plastic	Small decrease as more manufacturing firms invest in new computer and numerically controlled machinery and equipment, resulting in productivity increases.
Nursing aides, orderlies, and attendants	Small decrease in hospitals. Hospitals are delivering more acute-care services requiring highly trained personnel such as registered nurses, rather than nursing aides.
Order fillers, wholesale and retail trade	Small decrease reflecting productivity gains from electronic ordering systems which eliminate tasks requiring personal interaction.
Painters, transportation equipment	Small decrease in automotive repair shops and a small decrease in motor vehicle dealers because automobiles increasingly are expected to have plastic body panels, which are less likely to require repainting after minor collision damage. A significant decrease is expected in motor vehicles and equipment due to the increased use of robots to perform painting functions on assembly lines.
Physicians	Small decrease in offices of physicians due to the tendency toward large group practices, which require a higher proportion of nurses, technicians, and clerical support staff.
Plasterers	Small decrease reflecting the continuing replacement of plaster by drywall.
Police patrol officers	Small decrease in State government and a small increase in local government reflecting the trend for local areas to establish their own police departments.
Pressers, hand	Small decrease due to the growing impact of automation, resulting in productivity increases.
Real estate clerks	Small decrease reflecting the increasing use of computers, which will streamline many of the clerical tasks associated with real estate sales, property management, and recordkeeping.
Refuse collectors	Small decrease due to bigger, more efficient trucks and larger trash cans and bins, permitting less frequent collections.
Roustabouts	Small decrease due to continuing mechanization and introduction of new equipment, resulting in productivity increases.
Secretaries, except legal and medical	Small decrease reflecting the impact of office automation.
Service station attendants	Small decrease in gasoline service stations because of the trend toward self-service stations that do not provide maintenance services such as lubrication and accessory changes.
Sheriffs and deputy sheriffs	Small decrease because as suburbs continue to grow, more communities will have their own police department, which will perform many of the duties formerly done by sheriffs.
Signal or track switch maintainers	Small decrease due to increasing computerization and reliability of signals and switch controls.
Soldering and brazing machine operators and setters	Small decrease as firms continue to invest in new computer and numerically controlled machinery and automated material handling systems.
Statement clerks	Small decrease due to the growing automation of processing of customer bank accounts.
Stationary engineers	Small decrease due to the growing use of automated and computerized controls.
Stockclerks, stockroom, warehouse, or yard	Small decrease due to increasing automation such as computerized inventory control and automated material handling equipment.
Surveyors	Small decrease because the demand for surveying services is not expected to grow as rapidly as other services offered by industries which employ surveyors. In addition, technological innovations, such as the global positioning system, will result in productivity increases. A moderate increase is expected in miscellaneous business services because the demand for services provided by other workers in this industry is not growing as rapidly as demand for services provided by this occupation.

Expected Changes in Various Occupations

Occupation	Projected changes and reasons
Teachers and instructors, vocational education and training	Small decrease due to the fact that 80 percent of enrollees in vocational education are 18-34 years old and this population group is projected to decline through the year 2000.
Tire building machine operators	Small decrease due to expected productivity increases resulting from improved tire building machinery and equipment.
Tire repairers and changers	Small decrease in auto and home supply stores because the demand for services provided by other occupations in this industry is growing at a faster rate than the demand for services provided by this occupation.
Vehicle washers and equipment cleaners	Small decrease due to improved washing and cleaning equipment, resulting in productivity increases.
Watchmakers	Small decrease reflecting the trend towards disposable watches and clocks not requiring repair work.
Welders and cutters	Small decrease in manufacturing due to the increased use of robots and technological improvements.
Welding machine setters, operators, and tenders	Small decrease due to the increased use of robots to perform welding functions on assembly lines.
Moderate decrease	
Animal caretakers, except farm	Moderate decrease in agricultural services since the industries which employ these workers, such as animal and veterinary services, are not growing as fast as the other industries in this sector.
Bicycle repairers	Moderate decrease in miscellaneous shopping goods stores. The segment of the industry employing bicycle repairers is growing more slowly than other segments of this diverse industry because bicycle owners are increasingly performing most of their own repairs.
Billing, cost, and rate clerks	Moderate decrease due to continuing automation and productivity improvements.
Bookkeeping, accounting, and auditing clerks	Moderate decrease due to productivity increases brought about by computers and improved software.
Cement and gluing machine operators	Moderate decrease due to more advanced joining techniques and machinery.
Central office operators	Moderate decrease due to continuing automation of telephone central offices.
Chemical equipment controllers, operators, and tenders	Moderate decrease due to expected advances in computerized and automated control systems.
Chemical plant and systems operators	Moderate decrease because of increased automation and a trend toward larger plants controlled by the same number of workers.
Clinical laboratory technologists and technicians	Moderate decrease in hospitals because of efforts to contain costs and because of increasing reliance on medical laboratories for all but the most routine tests. A small increase is expected in medical and dental laboratories because they are increasingly switching to 24-hour service and are more able to afford new, expensive laboratory equipment.
College and university faculty	Moderate decrease in educational services because college and university enrollments are expected to decline as a proportion of total enrollments in educational services.
Compositors, typesetters, and arrangers, precision	Moderate decrease reflecting technological advances in computerized typesetting and an increase in investment centered on laborsaving equipment in typesetting, text layout, and automatic photo reproduction.
Cooking and roasting machine operators and tenders, food and tobacco	Moderate decrease due to the expected development of more efficient and advanced cooking and roasting equipment, resulting in increases in productivity.
Cooks, short order and fast food	Moderate decrease in eating and drinking places due to increasing average weekly work hours and slowing growth of the fast-food restaurant segment. Moderate increase in grocery stores as more prepared short-order and fast-food items are sold.
Crushing and mixing machine operators and tenders	Moderate decrease due to productivity increases resulting from the expected development of more highly automated and larger capacity crushing and mixing machinery.

Expected Changes in Various Occupations

Occupation	Projected changes and reasons
Cutting and slicing machine setters, operators, and tenders	Moderate decrease due to productivity increases resulting from the expected development of highly automated cutting and slicing machinery.
Duplicating, mail, and other office machine operators	Moderate decrease due to further advances in duplicating machine and mail handling technology and continuing office automation, such as the spreading use of electronic mail, copiers, and facsmile transmission.
Electrocardiographic technicians	Moderate decrease in hospitals reflecting an increasing use of multicompetent personnel, such as licensed practical nurses, as well as productivity increases due to new technology.
Electromechanical equipment assemblers, precision	Moderate decrease due to productivity increases resulting from technological improvements and automation.
Electronic home entertainment equipment repairers	Moderate decrease due to the lower maintenance requirements of equipment incorporating improved technology.
Electronic semiconductor processors	Moderate decrease due to increased efficiencies brought about by better use of technology and economies of scale.
Farm equipment mechanics	Moderate decrease in wholesale machinery, equipment, and supplies because the farm equipment dealer segment is expected to grow more slowly than the industry as a whole. A small increase is expected in crops, livestock, and livestock products reflecting trends toward larger farms and increasingly complex farm equipment.
Farm and home management advisors	Moderate decrease due to the projected decline in employment of farmers. No change is expected in electric utilities since this industry employs home management advisors who are not affected by the same factors as farm management advisors.
File clerks	Moderate decrease due to the growing use of electronic filing systems and optical disks as a storage medium.
Food counter, fountain, and related workers	Moderate decrease in eating and drinking places due to increasing average weekly work hours and slowing growth of the fast-food restaurant segment. Contracting out of food service functions should result in moderate decreases in education, hospitals, and personal care facilities.
Foundry mold assembly and shakeout workers	Moderate decrease reflecting the continued trend toward automation in the steel industry.
Furnace, kiln, or kettle operators and tenders	Moderate decrease due to the productivity increases resulting from the expected development of more highly automated and larger capacity furnaces, kilns, and kettles.
Gas and petroleum plant and system occupations	Moderate decrease due to increased automation and a trend toward larger plants operated by the same number of workers.
Grinders and polishers, hand	Moderate decrease due to expected productivity increases resulting from more advanced grinding and polishing machines.
Handpackers and packagers	Moderate decrease due to productivity increases resulting from the use of improved tools and equipment.
Home appliance and power tool repairers	Moderate decrease reflecting the lower maintenance requirements of appliances and tools incorporating improved technology. A significant decrease is expected in department stores as they continue to eliminate appliance repair departments for competitive reasons.
Jewelers and silversmiths	Moderate decrease in miscellaneous shopping goods stores because jewelry stores, where this occupation is concentrated, are growing at a much slower rate than the industry as a whole.
Letterpress operators	Moderate decrease due to the replacement of letterpress printing by newer and faster printing technology.
Library assistants and bookmobile drivers	Moderate decrease in local government due to increasing library automation and the use of computers to handle the growing volume of information.
Machine assemblers	Moderate decrease reflecting increasing use of robots and highly automated production technology as well as the trend toward moving assembly to low-wage countries.
Machine builders and other precision machine assemblers	Moderate decrease due to productivity increases resulting from technological improvements and automation.
Machine feeders and offbearers	Moderate decrease due to improved machinery and equipment that can automatically load and unload.
Machine forming operators and tenders, metal and plastic	Moderate decrease due to the greater use of computer-controlled equipment.

Expected Changes in Various Occupations

Occupation	Projected changes and reasons
Mail clerks, except mail machine operators and postal service	Moderate decrease due to continuing automation, including robotics and electronic mail, which more firms will be able to afford.
Messengers	Moderate decrease due to the growing use of facsimile machines and computer data transmission.
Metal pourers and casters, basic shapes	Moderate decrease due to productivity increases resulting from new casting technologies, such as continuous casting.
Meter readers, utilities	Moderate decrease due to the development of remote meter reading.
Musical instrument repairers and tuners	Moderate decrease in appliance, radio, TV, and music stores because employment in music stores is not expected to increase as rapidly as employment in other parts of this industry.
Office machine and cash register servicers	Moderate decrease reflecting the trend towards computerized office machines, which are repaired by computer service technicians.
Optometrists	Moderate decrease in offices of "other health practitioners" reflecting a shift in optometrist services to retail outlets.
Order clerks, materials, merchandise, and service	Moderate decrease as office automation increases, including the capability to transmit orders electronically.
Packaging and filling machine operators and tenders	Moderate decrease due to expected productivity increases resulting from new packaging techniques.
Painting, coating, and decorating workers, hand	Moderate decrease due to changes in technology and business practices. A small increase is expected in household furniture; glass and glassware; watches and clocks; and jewelry, silverware, and flatware because of the demand for fine quality, hand-finished products, which are unlikely to be affected by advances in technology or automation.
Payroll and timekeeping clerks	Moderate decrease due to continuing automation, such as computerized payroll systems and electronic timeclocks.
Pest controllers and assistants	Moderate decrease in service to dwellings and other buildings because the demand for services provided by other workers in this industry is growing more rapidly than demand for services provided by this occupation.
Photographic processing machine operators and tenders	Moderate decrease in miscellaneous business services because the demand for services provided by other workers in this industry is growing more rapidly than demand for services provided by this occupation.
Physician assistants	Moderate decrease because relatively few applicants and graduates from physician assistant programs are expected to be available, resulting in employers either doing without physician assistants or substituting nurse practitioners instead.
Printing press machine operators and tenders	Moderate decrease in commercial and business forms due to the improvements in high-speed web-offset presses, which require less labor to run. A small decrease is expected in newspapers as technological improvements to printing presses have reduced labor requirements.
Public relations specialists	Moderate decrease in miscellaneous business services because the demand for services provided by other workers in this industry is growing more rapidly than demand for services provided by this occupation.
Separating and still machine operators and tenders	Moderate decrease due to technological advances in machines that sort, separate, and extract materials, such as filter presses, centrifuges, and evaporating tanks.
Shoe sewing machine operators and tenders	Moderate decrease reflecting the adverse effects of rising shoe imports and productivity increases resulting from advances in stitching machines.
Solderers and brazers	Moderate decrease because of increasing automation and subsequent productivity increases.
Title examiners and searchers	Moderate decrease in pension funds and insurance due to the increasing use of computers to access title information.
Wholesale and retail buyers, except farm products	Moderate decrease due to the rise in mergers and acquisitions, which force firms to drop excess staff. There is also a trend toward manufacturers shipping directly to the retailer, which decreases the demand for buyers. A small decrease is expected in grocery stores since these two factors do not affect this industry as much as other industries.

Expected Changes in Various Occupations

Occupation	Projected changes and reasons
Significant decrease	
Billing, posting, and calculating machine operators	Significant decrease as improved computer technology enables billing clerks and other related workers to take over machine operating duties.
Broadcast technicians	Significant decrease due to the development of automated equipment and the trend for maintenance work to be done by equipment repairers rather than broadcast technicians.
Brokerage clerks	Significant decrease due to productivity increases resulting from the impact of office automation such as word and data processing for computation and recordkeeping.
Central office and PBX installers and repairers	Significant decrease due to the increased use of technology which permits more telephone signals per wire as well as advances in switching technology which increase capacity and reliability.
Data entry keyers, composing	Significant decrease reflecting the growing use of personal computers by reporters, editors, and others in newspapers and miscellaneous publishing.
Data entry keyers, except composing	Significant decrease as improvements to data entry technologies result in productivity increases and as data entry is increasingly being done by professionals through the use of personal computers.
Dental laboratory technicians, precision	Significant decrease in medical and dental laboratories because dental laboratories will grow much more slowly than medical laboratories.
Directory assistance operators	Significant decrease due to continuing office automation, increased centralization of telephone operations, and the decreased demand for services arising from charges for assistance.
Electrical and electronic equipment assemblers, precision	Significant decrease reflecting the increasing use of robots or other automated processes in electronic assembly and the shift of assembly operations to low-wage countries.
Frame wirers, central office	Significant decrease due to the increased use of microelectronics that permit more telephone signals to be transmitted per wire. The use of modular connections rather than soldering will also reduce employment requirements.
Nuclear engineers	Significant decrease in engineering and architectural services because no new nuclear power plants are expected to be ordered before the year 2000. A significant decrease is also expected in miscellaneous business services because the demand for services provided by this occupation is growing at a slower rate than the demand for services provided by other occupations in this industry.
Podiatrists	Signficant decrease in offices of "other health practitioners" because demand for services provided by other occupations in this industry is growing at a faster rate than the demand for services of podiatrists.
Proofreaders and copy markers	Significant decrease due to computerization and more sophisticated software programs.
Station installers and repairers, telephone	Significant decrease as telephones are cheaper to replace than repair and pre-wired outlets allow consumers to connect their own phones.
Statistical clerks	Significant decrease due to increased computerization, which provides an expanding number of statistical programs for users.
Stenographers	Significant decrease due to the proliferation of increasingly sophisticated dictation equipment. No change is expected in Federal, State, and local governments since these industries will continue to need written transcripts for various legal purposes.
Telephone and cable TV line installers and repairers	Significant decrease in telephone communications reflecting the switch from the traditional type of lines to microwave transmission, as well as the greater efficiency obtained from using fiber optic cable. A moderate decrease is expected in telegraph and communications services due to the limited number of additional households expected to subscribe to cable TV after the mid-1990's.
Typists and word processors	Significant decrease due to productivity improvements resulting from expansion of office automation and the increased use of word processing equipment by professionals. No change is expected in personnel supply services because of the continuing demand for temporary workers.

Expected Changes in Various Industries

Industry	Assumptions
Agricultural services, forestry, and fishing	Demand for agricultural services will be strong, especially for landscaping services.
Coal mining	Increased use of coal as a fuel for the generation of electricity assumed. Production assumptions based on Department of Energy forecasts.
Crude petroleum, natural gas, and gas liquids	Higher prices, efficiency in the use of energy, and advances in the production and transmission of electricity will keep petroleum demand at moderate levels. Foreign sources are projected to supply an increasing portion of demand; domestic production is projected to decline. These assumptions are based on Department of Energy forecasts.
Oil and gas field services	Increases in the price of petroleum will encourage increases in the exploration of domestic sources.
Nonmetallic minerals, except fuels	Growth in the construction industries will translate into growth for the products of this industry.
New nonfarm housing	Single and multifamily housing construction will slow from rates of early 1980's because of the expected slowdown in new household formation.
New industrial buildings	Growth projected for new factory construction. Modernization of existing facilities will also be prevalent.
New commercial buildings	Office and other commercial buildings are expected to recover from recent oversupply, but future growth will be slower than during the building boom of 1983-85.
New educational buildings	After years of decline, new school construction will continue to swing upward at a modest pace, reflecting growth in the school-age population.
New hospitals and institutions	Increases expected in both hospital and nursing home construction.
New electric utility facilities	Expenditures expected to continue to move upward following 1979-85 cutbacks.
New water supply and sewer facilities	Increased demand for sewage treatment plants and waste disposal facilities was assumed.
New roads	Replacement of aging bridges and highways will lead to continued growth of road construction.
Logging camps and logging contractors	Growth in the paper products industries as well as increases in residential construction will lead to increased demand for logging, although at a slower pace than in the past.
Sawmills and planing mills	Growth in construction will lead to moderate growth in this industry.
Millwork and structural wood members, nec	Structure of industry does not permit extensive automation. Demand for this industry's products depends mainly on new residential construction and the repair/remodeling sector.
Household furniture	Personal consumption requirements will grow moderately.
Partitions and fixtures	Increase in demand caused by capital spending by the trade sector.
Office and miscellaneous furniture and fixtures	Increase in demand due to investment. Demand for new office furniture will be strong. No significant technological advances in production processes expected for this sector.
Glass and glass products	Continued decline in use of glass for packaging foods and beverages is expected.
Concrete, gypsum, and plaster products	Little technological change expected.
Blast furnaces and basic steel products	Slack demand will result in only slight growth for this industry. Imports will continue to hold about 20 percent of the market. Minimills will take a larger share of U.S. steel business. Imports will be mainly of semifinished steel, to be processed in U.S. finishing mills.
Primary aluminum	Production declines will halt since most of the more inefficient mills have closed.
Copper rolling and drawing	The substitution of other materials and the growth of fiber optics and satellite communications will result in slow growth for this industry.
Aluminum rolling and drawing	This industry is expected to grow slowly since other materials will be substituted for aluminum.
Metal cans and shipping containers	Continued relative decline in use of metal cans as a packaging material for many foods and beverages due to use of plastics and increase in microwave and frozen foods.

Expected Changes in Various Industries

Industry	Assumptions
Fabricated structural metal products	Growth of construction will lead to growth of this industry. Some gain in exports also expected.
Screw machine products, bolts, rivets, etc	This industry will continue to grow due to increasing demand for capital equipment.
Automotive stampings	Slowdown in motor vehicle and truck production will limit growth in this industry.
Stampings, except automotive	Growth expected in intermediate demand for appliance and computer casings. Technological advances and diffusion are likely to come slowly since much of this industry consists of small job shops.
Metal coating, engraving, and allied services	Productivity growth limited by the large number of small firms in the industry and product diversity.
Ordnance, except vehicles and missiles	Defense requirements assumed to be lower than in 1986.
Miscellaneous fabricated metal products	Productivity gains from past technological advances will not be repeated as technology has already spread to much of the industry. Much of the industry's output is custom made, which limits productivity gains from economies of scale.
Engines and turbines	Many of this industry's products are specially designed, particularly for ships and power generating units, limiting productivity advances. Imports are expected to increase their market share slightly. Exports will recover due to a lower exchange rate.
Farm and garden machinery	Demand expected to increase as a result of capital spending by the real estate and farming sectors. Exports are expected to recover due to a lower exchange rate.
Construction machinery	Increased purchases due to investment. Demand should be strong because of maintenance of the Nation's infrastructure. Exports are expected to recover due to lower exchange rate. Producing factories are already heavily mechanized; productivity gains associated with plant closings are not foreseen.
Mining and oil field machinery	Some increases in oil exploration stemming from higher oil prices should boost demand for oil field machinery. Productivity growth limited because of the custom-designed nature of the equipment of this sector.
Materials handling machinery and equipment	Increased factory automation, leading to increased investment expenditures, will stimulate this sector. Exports should show strong growth due to lower exchange rate.
Special industry machinery	The food, paper, printing, and rubber industries buy investment goods from this industry. Imports made permanent inroads in this industry's markets, and it is unlikely U.S. producers can fully recover these markets. Exports should show strong growth due to lower exchange rate.
General industrial machinery	Growth due to general growth of economy and exports. Investment expenditures also should increase.
Electronic computing equipment	Technological advances in the personal computer market are expected to continue to make systems more capable and easier to use. All industries are projected to have very strong investment demand for computer equipment. Computer-aided design, flexible manufacturing systems, and computer-integrated manufacturing will affect all areas of manufacturing. Both exports and imports are expected to have strong gains; a favorable net balance of trade for the United States is expected for this industry.
Office and accounting machines	Demand for investment goods from the trade, finance, and service sectors will contribute to growth.
Electrical industrial apparatus	Most of the demand for the products of this industry is from mature markets—mainly appliances and industrial machinery and equipment. As a result, there is little potential for rapid growth.
Household appliances	No major new products comparable to the microwave are presently under development. Appliances will have more microprocessors, replacing electromechanical controls. Productivity improvements are likely; there are many hand assemblers, and many products can be standardized. The industry could use robots and other automation methods. Imports will grow as a share, but will not dominate. A lower exchange rate will contribute to increased export competitiveness.
Electronic home entertainment equipment	The consumer electronics market is projected to continue the trend of very high levels of demand. Consumers will upgrade their existing systems by purchasing such items as super VCR's, wider screen TV sets, and compact disc players. It is assumed that much of the production and assembly of this equipment will be done overseas; the domestic industry will be concentrated on management and research and development. Growth in high-priced stereo equipment in motor vehicles will also help to fuel growth of this industry.
Telephone and telegraph apparatus	The communications sector will buy investment goods from this industry, which will continue to be very healthy because of the increasing need for telecommunications equipment. Imports will increase, and a lower exchange rate will contribute to strong export growth.

Expected Changes in Various Industries

Industry	Assumptions
Radio and TV communication equipment	Increases in civilian requirements will offset decreases in defense demand. Increased sophistication of other machinery and equipment requires higher purchases of communications equipment as an input. Future growth will be attributable to the private sector. There will be more private purchases of satellites, fiber optic systems, and equipment related to telecommunications. Impact of high definition TV will not be felt in this century.
Electronic tubes	Growth expected despite continued substitution of solid-state devices and semiconductors.
Semiconductors and related devices	More equipment and instruments will have electronic components. There are some limits to growth as this industry matures and imports rise, but domestic production will still expand rapidly. The United States will still lead in the development of specialized chips.
X-ray and other electromedical apparatus	The health industries buy investment goods from this sector; demand is assumed to be especially strong because of the aging of the population and advances in biotechnology.
Motor vehicles and parts	A slow growth in auto purchases reflects a projected slowdown in the growth of the driving-age population. Many foreign car manufacturers are assumed to open plants in the U.S., leading to a leveling off in the import share of output. Some import growth is expected from the Third World. Labor productivity will continue to grow.
Aircraft	Defense demand is expected to decline; the slack will be taken up by exports and investment purchases.
Aircraft and missile engines and equipment	Defense demand is expected to decline. Exports are expected to show strong growth.
Guided missiles and space vehicles	Defense spending assumed to grow slowly, maintaining the posture attained during the 1980's buildup. Exports will show strong growth.
Ship and boat building and repairing	Defense spending assumed to be lower than in the 1980's. Boat building for the consumer market will take up the slack.
Engineering and scientific instruments	Increased demand due to investment (especially for research and development) and strong growth of exports.
Measuring and controlling devices	Demand will be dependent on investment, especially by public utilities, and by exports. More instruments and equipment will incorporate automatic sensors.
Optical and ophthalmic products	Growth in demand caused by investment by the chemical and health services sectors, and by exports. Demand will be high, especially for spectrographs and electron microscopes. Personal consumption expenditures will grow due to the fast-growing older population, which requires more vision care, and the increased popularity of contact lenses.
Medical instruments and supplies	Increased demand because of high investment by health services.
Photographic equipment and supplies	Increased demand will result from the capital needs of the trade and service sectors and from consumer expenditures. Advances in technology will lead to continued purchases of new equipment.
Watches, clocks, and parts	Imports will dominate, leading to a decline for the domestic industry.
Jewelry, silverware, and plated ware	Continued growth of imported goods will lead to slow growth for the domestic industry.
Toys and sporting goods	Output will continue to grow despite the growth of imports.
Meat products	Slow growth of meat products due to slower population growth and less meat consumption. Poultry will increasingly replace pork and beef for health reasons. Productivity will continue to increase, but at a much slower rate because mechanization and assembly line speed are reaching limits.
Dairy products	Slow growth is expected. Health concerns expected to lead movement to low-fat products.
Canned, dried, and frozen foods	Demand will be very strong for dried or frozen specialties but weak for canned goods. By 2000, virtually all homes will have a microwave oven.
Grain mill products and fats and oils	Health concerns will boost demand for grain products.
Sugar and confectionery products	Health concerns will lead to a relative decrease in the use of sugar as an ingredient in prepared foods.
Alcoholic beverages	Consumers are expected to continue to drink less alcoholic beverages per capita.
Soft drinks and flavorings	The slower growth of the teenage population will limit demand for soft drinks. Some increase expected as consumers substitute soft drinks for alcoholic beverages.

Expected Changes in Various Industries

Industry	Assumptions
Tobacco manufactures	Health concerns and antismoking campaigns will cause the sales of tobacco to decline.
Weaving, finishing, yarn, and thread mills	Already heavily mechanized, but automated production technologies will become more widespread.
Knitting mills	Industry already heavily automated; domestic producers very competitive with importers.
Apparel	Consumer demand will grow somewhat faster than population due to rising income levels, but more of it will be met by imports. Domestic production will increase slightly.
Pulp, paper, and paperboard mills	Continued growth of paper products and printing and publishing industries will lead to growth. Industry will continue to have strong productivity growth.
Miscellaneous publishing	Production will be high due to the growth of catalogs, directories, newsletters, technical manuals, and other types of miscellaneous publishing.
Commercial printing and business forms	Firms will continue to increase their purchases of commercial printing and business forms; desk-top publishing will not have a dramatic impact.
Industrial chemicals	Disposal of toxic wastes will be a troublesome problem for the industry.
Plastics materials and synthetics	Some output growth as plastics continue to substitute for metals (for example, carbon fiber resin in autos and airplanes). However, growth will be somewhat dampened by slowdown in synthetic fibers as apparel production slows.
Drugs	Strong long-term growth is projected due to a strong demand for established drugs, a vast array of new products, and an expanding elderly population. Biotechnology advances for both humans and animals are expected to contribute to the number of products available. Strong export growth assumed.
Paints and allied products	Slower growth in construction and motor vehicle sectors will lead to slowdown in this industry.
Agricultural chemicals	Virtually no growth despite gains in farm output. This reflects the continued decline in the relative input of agricultural chemicals, as consumers and growers alike become increasingly wary of the environmental and health problems associated with some of these products. Growth due to growth of exports.
Petroleum refining	Industries will continue energy conservation measures in an attempt to control costs. Vehicles will become more energy efficient. The use of coal for electric generation will increase. Production projections based on assumptions of Department of Energy.
Miscellaneous plastic products	Growth will slow as substitution of plastic products for metal and glass reaches saturation. Introduction of biodegradable plastics may spur growth.
Footwear except rubber and plastic	Output will decline as imports continue to increase.
Luggage, handbags, and leather products, nec	Little output change as imports continue to increase.
Water transportation	Continued relative decline in shipping as means of transporting goods to market.
Air transportation	Demand for air travel will continue to grow rapidly despite safety concerns and already congested airports. Significant increase in consumer demand reflects growth in discretionary income and an increase in the number of senior citizens.
Pipe lines, except natural gas	Energy conservation and higher imports of crude petroleum products will lead to continued growth for this industry.
Arrangement of passenger transportation	As a result of airline deregulation and the growth in the number of fares for all modes of transportation, growth will continue in the use of travel agents as persons and businesses find it increasingly difficult to make their own travel arrangements.
Communications except broadcasting	Telephone services are expected to show rapid growth with applications and extensions of current technology. Productivity will be high, leading to little job growth.
Radio and television broadcasting	The increasing popularity of cable TV is expected to continue as the industry makes an effort to develop better programs. There are limits to growth in this sector as cable TV approaches market saturation. Advertising revenues will continue to spur growth of this sector. Employment will expand in sales and service.
Electric utilities including combined services	The shift away from oil and natural gas in home heating and towards electricity is expected to continue. Demand for electric utilities is expected to grow more rapidly than demand for other energy sources. Growth will be slower than in the past, based on the assumptions of the Department of Energy. Conservation of energy will continue.

Expected Changes in Various Industries

Industry	Assumptions
Gas utilities including combined services	Continued energy conservation measures will decrease relative use of natural gas by all industries. This assumption is based on estimates by the Department of Energy.
Water and sanitation including combined services	This industry is expected to grow due to general growth of the economy and to increasing demand for refuse and waste disposal.
Retail trade, except eating and drinking places	Retailers will have difficulty finding part-time workers; past declines in the workweek will taper. Grocery stores will be faced with increading pressure to raise productivity, but at the same time they will offer more labor-intensive services (salad bars, prepared foods, deli's, etc.), and more grocery stores will extend hours. Teleshopping is not assumed to have a major impact on retailers through 2000.
Eating and drinking places	Fast-food growth will slow. The decline in the youth population will also affect fast-food restaurants as employers—about half their workers are young people. The increasing popularity of microwave ovens and the availability of prepared meals from grocery and specialty stores are other reasons to explain the slowdown in food-away-from-home sales. Full-service restaurants are expected to grow as well as contracting for food service operations by hospitals, schools, and other institutions.
Banking	Wider use of automatic banking and electronic funds transfers assumed. Productivity will be high as office automation reduces the need for large numbers of clerical workers.
Security and commodity brokers and exchanges	Personal spending on brokerage charges and investment counseling has undergone tremendous growth recently. Growth is expected to continue, although the projected growth rate is not expected to match that of recent years. Consumers will increase their demand for financial planning advice. Other growth will come from expanding pension funds, college endowments, and retirement programs such as IRA and Keogh; under deregulation, brokerage firms can offer more financial and credit services.
Insurance services	Greater efficiencies assumed in computerized underwriting for standardized life insurance policies. Increasing demand assumed for specialized insurance, such as accident and health or fire and casualty, which is not easily standardized. Work force may have to increase because of the demand for new commercial coverage such as product liability, prepaid legal, or pollution liability. Noninsurance firms (such as banks and department stores) may take away some of the insurance industry's business, but this should be partially offset by expansion of insurance firms into other financial services.
Hotels and other lodging places	Personal expenditures are expected to outstrip business expenditures as more discretionary income and more senior citizens lead to increased vacation expenditures.
Personal services, nec	An expanding array of new personal services such as diet workshops and buyers' clubs assumed; demand expected to be high due to two-earner families.
Advertising	Businesses will spend relatively more on advertising as they continue their attempt to extend markets in an increasingly competitive environment.
Services to dwellings and other buildings	Businesses will increase their expenditures on these services as building managers continue to contract out for many of these services, especially those performed on an irregular basis. Higher government purchases of contract cleaning services assumed.
Personnel supply services	Businesses will increase their expenditures, especially for temporary help services. They will continue their use of employment agencies in an attempt to find the best qualified jobseekers. The market for temporaries will expand even further beyond office clerical workers to include more nursing, engineering, and industrial workers. More contracts for facilities management on the part of government assumed.
Computer and data processing services	Business expenditures will increase as firms attempt to find the right software to fill their needs, and as specialized software is designed and developed. Strong government demand assumed.
Research, management, and consulting services	Businesses will increase expenditures as they continue to contract out for specialized services, especially market research, personnel training, management, efficiency experts, lobbyists, and other business consultants. In the future, industrial R&D should grow faster than Federal. Government agencies are assumed to contract out for more managerial and consulting services.
Detective and protective services	Business and government will continue to increase their expenditures for these services. However, as the industry matures, guard services are not expected to grow as rapidly as in the past. Some additional growth will come from the sale and operation of security systems.
Credit reporting and business services, nec	Business expenditures on miscellaneous services are expected to increase as the number of services expands.
Electrical repair shops	Growth in consumer demand is expected to continue.
Theatrical producers and entertainers	Output will be stimulated by the increased programming required for cable television.

Expected Changes in Various Industries

Industry	Assumptions
Bowling alleys and billiard establishments	Decreasing consumer expenditures are projected to continue.
Amusement and recreation services, nec	Consumer demand will be very high.
Offices of health practitioners	More health services will be performed in offices and group practice centers rather than in hospitals.
Nursing and personal care facilities	Fueling the demand for nursing homes and skilled-care nursing facilities will be strong growth in the elderly population (especially those over age 85). Increased cost-consciousness by hospitals will shift many patients to nursing homes.
Hospitals, private	Growth will be slowed by cost-containment pressures which force a shift of services from hospitals to doctors' offices and outpatient facilities, but new technologies and an older population will keep demand high.
Outpatient facilities and health services, nec	The growing elderly population, the shorter length of stay in hospitals, and the lower cost of home health care will result in more outpatient visits and increased demand for home care services.
Legal services	Increased litigation and the trend toward more specialized services and regional expansion of law firms will boost output.
Educational services, private	Spending will increase moderately despite slow growth in the college-age population due to higher enrollments of older students and minorities. Vocational programs will grow.
Individual and miscellaneous social services.	Demand and employment are projected to grow rapidly (although slower than during 1976-88), especially for counseling, senior services, and fundraising activities. Growth will be driven by insurance reimbursement for counseling services; lack of jail space, which will force other types of rehabilitative efforts; and mandatory counseling for drivers convicted of driving while intoxicated.
Child day care services	Growth will occur as more mothers enter the work force and care shifts from home-based babysitting to the commercial sector. Growth is projected to slow due to a decline in the under-5 population.
Residential care	This sector will be affected by the shift away from hospital care. Strong growth is expected for drug and alcohol rehabilitation centers and elderly residential care.
Private households	Demand for housekeeping and babysitting will grow, but will be met more by contract firms than by private individuals.
Engineering and architectural services	As buildings become more complex, and zoning and building codes more demanding, the construction industry will increase its purchases of these services. Other industries, especially in manufacturing, will also increase their purchases of engineering services.
Accounting, auditing, and services, nec	The continued complexity of tax laws, accounting procedures, and reporting requirements will cause increased expenditures by business for these services.
U.S. Postal Service	Innovations in letter-processing equipment will hold down employment.

BOOKS FOR JOB HUNTERS

CAREERS / STUDY GUIDES

Airline Pilot
Allied Health Professions
Federal Jobs for College Graduates
Federal Jobs in Law Enforcement
Getting Started in Film
How to Pass Clerical Employment Tests
How You Really Get Hired
Make Your Job Interview a Success
Mechanical Aptitude and Spatial Relations Tests
Mid-Career Job Hunting
100 Best Careers for the Year 2000
Passport to Overseas Employment
Travel Agent
You as a Law Enforcement Officer

RESUME GUIDES

The Complete Resume Guide
Resumes for Better Jobs
Resumes That Get Jobs
Your Resume: Key to a Better Job

AVAILABLE AT BOOKSTORES EVERYWHERE

PRENTICE HALL

CIVIL SERVICE BOOKS

TEST PREPARATION

Accountant / Auditor
ACWA: Administrative Careers With America
Air Traffic Controller Qualifying Test
Air Traffic Controller Training Program
American Foreign Service Officer
Assistant Accountant
Beginning Clerical Worker
Bookkeeper / Account Clerk
Building Custodian / Building Superintendent /
    Custodian Engineer
Bus Operator / Conductor
Case Worker
Computer Specialist GS 5-9
The Corey Guide to Postal Exams
Correction Officer
Correction Officer Promotion Tests
Court Officer / Senior Court Officer / Court Clerk
Distribution Clerk, Machine
Drug Enforcement Agent
Electrician / Electrician's Helper
Emergency Dispatcher / 911 Operator
Federal Clerk / Steno / Typist
File Clerk / General Clerk
Fire Department Lieutenant / Captain /
    Battalion Chief
Firefighter
Gardener / Grounds Maintenance Worker
Investigator / Claim Examiner
Machinist / Machinist's Helper
Mail Handler / Mail Processor
Maintenance Worker / Mechanical Maintainer
Mark-up Clerk / Clerk Typist /
    Clerk Stenographer—U.S. Postal Service
Office Aide
Office Associate
Plumber / Steam Fitter
Police Administrative Aide
Police Officer
Police Sergeant / Lieutenant / Captain
Postal Exams Handbook
Post Office Clerk / Carrier

Preparación para el Examen de Cartero
Principal Administrative Associate /
    Administrative Assistant
Principal Clerk / Principal Stenographer
Probation Officer / Parole Officer
Rural Carrier
Sanitation Worker
Senior Clerical Series
Special Agent
Special Officer / Senior Special Officer /
    Bridge and Tunnel Officer
Staff Analyst / Associate Staff Analyst
State Trooper / Highway Patrol Officer /
    State Traffic Officer
Track Worker
Traffic Enforcement Agent
Train Operator / Tower Operator / Assistant
    Train Dispatcher

CAREERS / STUDY GUIDES

Civil Service Administrative Tests
Civil Service Arithmetic and Vocabulary
Civil Service Clerical Promotion Tests
Civil Service Handbook
Civil Service Psychological and Psychiatric
    Tests
Civil Service Reading Comprehension Tests
Civil Service Tests for Basic Skills Jobs
Complete Guide to U.S. Civil Service Jobs
Federal Jobs for College Graduates
Federal Jobs in Law Enforcement
General Test Practice for 101 U.S. Jobs
How to Get a Clerical Job in Government
New York City Civil Service Job Guide
101 Challenging Government Jobs for
    College Graduates
Practice for Clerical, Typing and
    Stenographic Tests
SF 171: The Federal Employment
    Application Form
Supervision
You as a Law Enforcement Officer

AVAILABLE AT BOOKSTORES EVERYWHERE

PRENTICE HALL